Theodore Dreiser's "Heard in the Corridors"
Articles and Related Writings

Theodore Dreiser's

"Heard in the Corridors" Articles
and
Related Writings

EDITED BY

T. D. Nostwich

Iowa State University Press / Ames

T. D. Nostwich is Associate Professor of English, Iowa State University.

Composed by Iowa State University Press
Printed in the United States of America

First edition, 1988

Library of Congress Cataloging-in-Publication Data

Dreiser, Thedore, 1871–1945.
  Theodore Dreiser's "Heard in the corridors" articles and related writings.

  1. Imaginary conversations. 2. Interviews – United States. I. Nostwich, T. D., 1925–   . II. Title.
PS3507.R55A6   1988   814′.52   87–13095
ISBN 0–8138–1737–4

FRONTISPIECE: The Theodore Dreiser Collection, Department of Special Collections, Van Pelt Library, University of Pennsylvania.

Contents

Preface / ix
Introduction / xiii

CHICAGO DAILY GLOBE
"About the Hotels"

St. Louis Globe-Democrat
"Gossip of Chicago's Big Show"

"Heard in the Corridors"

TITLED INTERVIEWS

𝔗𝔥𝔢 ℌ𝔦𝔱𝔱𝔰𝔟𝔲𝔯𝔤 𝔇𝔦𝔰𝔭𝔞𝔱𝔠𝔥

Preface

THE material of this book is a segment of a larger complete edition of Theodore Dreiser's newspaper stories written from 1892 through 1895 that I have edited but which in its entirety of more than 2300 pages has proved too expensive to publish, given the unfortunate reality of today's printing costs. This segment, however, consisting of Dreiser's "Heard in the Corridors" articles and a number of related pieces, presents in a short volume what is perhaps his most significant journalism, his earliest creative work, which, as he said, gave him the opportunity to test his wings as an imaginative writer—more so, indeed, than any of his other reportorial assignments.

None of the pieces reprinted here had bylines. They are attributed to Dreiser on the basis of (*a*) internal evidence that establishes his unquestionable or highly probable authorship, i.e., the presence of names, happenings, or characteristic attitudes closely associated with him and referred to elsewhere in his writings or in writings about him; (*b*) inclusion among the ninety-six "Corridors" paragraphs that he preserved on five large (9″ x 14¼″) loose scrapbook-type pages now contained in File 86 of the Dreiser Collection at the University of Pennsylvania. Inclusion of a paragraph in File 86 is assumed to be sufficient evidence of his authorship, and therefore no attribution note is given for it. Each of the seventy-nine items not found in that file has an individual or group note stating the rationale for the attribution. Since none of these items except for Nos. 169–75 was originally given a separate title, the table of contents lists each by the name of the speaker being interviewed or, in the few instances where the speaker is not named, by the first few words of the piece.

The source of these articles is the newspapers in which they originally appeared. No other copy-texts are known to exist. The *Chicago Daily Globe* items, Nos. 1–4, are reprinted from the unique file owned by the Chicago Public Library. The *St. Louis Globe-Democrat* items, Nos. 5–171, are reprinted from microfilm owned by the Library of Congress. The *Pittsburg Dispatch* items, Nos. 172–75, are reprinted from microfilm owned by the Center for Research Libraries in Chicago.

The texts are reproduced exactly as they appear in the newspapers except for the correction of spelling and punctuation errors and the insertion of missing letters or words. Apart from two instances explained in the textual notes for items 37 and 47, my emendations are so slight in nature that they do not merit citation here. A complete list of them — eighty-seven in all — is, however, on file in the Dreiser Collection of the University of Pennsylvania Library. Old-fashioned spellings sanctioned by the *OED* or *Webster's Second* or *Third International Dictionaries* have been preserved without comment. On the assumption that Dreiser may have been recording a person's actual speech, grammatical errors such as dangling modifiers and disagreements of subject and predicate have not been corrected. Notes have been supplied to clarify obscure passages, identify some of the people mentioned, or correct errors of fact. The notes are labeled by article number and by the number of the line within the article.

I wish to thank the University of Pennsylvania for permission to quote from manuscript material in its possession and Harold J. Dies of the Dreiser Trust for permission to quote from *Dawn, A Hoosier Holiday, Newspaper Days,* and *Twelve Men.*

I am much indebted to Neda M. Westlake, former curator of the Charles Patterson Van Pelt Library Rare Book Collection, not only for making the vast University of Pennsylvania Dreiser Collection accessible to me but for her kind assistance, encouragement, and advice over several years.

My work was greatly expedited by the microfilm of the *St. Louis Globe-Democrat* loaned me by the Library of Congress and by the microfilm of the *Pittsburg Dispatch* loaned me by the Center for Research Libraries in Chicago.

I am grateful to Joy Gleason and her staff at the Newspaper and General Periodicals Center of the Chicago Public Library for expending much time and effort in tracing volumes of the *Chicago Daily Globe.*

Several staff members of the Iowa State University Library took a kind interest in the progress of my work and assisted me in innumerable ways. I wish particularly to thank Elaine Campbell, Donald Pady, and Susan Rafter.

Completion of this edition was facilitated by generous assistance in the form of released time and grants-in-aid from the Iowa State University College of Sciences and Humanities and the Graduate College.

The Iowa State University English Department was especially helpful in providing me with research assignments, research assistants, and funds for the reproduction of microfilmed material.

Thomas P. Riggio read the work in manuscript and made many perceptive, helpful comments on it.

I am deeply grateful for the encouragement and assistance of two good friends and colleagues, Richard Herrnstadt and Keith Huntress.

My labors were lightened by the following people who made proofreading almost a pleasure: Jane Nolan, Ann and Elisabeth Nostwich, Janet Searls, and Sunanda Vittal.

Assuredly I could not have completed this book without the sympathy and forbearance of my wife Ann, to whom I dedicate that portion of it which is my own.

Introduction

Theodore Dreiser's contributions to a daily newspaper column called "Heard in the Corridors," written when he was a young reporter for the *St. Louis Globe-Democrat,* November 1892 through April 1893, are gathered here, together with some other closely related pieces. Ostensibly the comments of local hotel guests, most of these paragraphs are actually the fabrications of Dreiser himself. Many are anecdotes, and many are short essays. The principal value of these little compositions lies in their being the novelist's earliest known creative work and in their anticipation of themes and topics in his later, more mature writing. Slight though their intrinsic literary merit may be, they can be read as a kind of table talk, enjoyable for their many curious sidelights on life of the early 1890s.

"Heard in the Corridors" was one of several newspaper features devised by Joseph Burbridge McCullagh (1842–96), the *St. Louis Globe-Democrat*'s most famous editor.[1] Under McCullagh's direction, which began in 1875, the paper became one of the best known in the nation and certainly the most widely read in the Mississippi Valley and the Southwest. A brilliant innovator who constantly sought improved methods of newsgathering and novel ways to capture reader interest, McCullagh made heavy use of the formal interview, a technique he virtually invented. He was the first reporter to interview a United States president (Andrew Johnson at the time of his impeachment), out of which deed grew the modern presidential press conference. As editor of the *Globe-Democrat* he often mobilized teams of reporters to gather the opinions of people attending professional, trade, church, and political conventions. Several full pages were often required to print these mass interviews.

From occasional coverage of this sort he went on to weekly group interviews. For example, one such feature, "About Old People," ran brief summaries of the activities and thoughts of elderly St. Louisans. Another, "Local Gossip," a staple item for many years on the Sunday editorial page, provided a forum for a dozen or more ordinary or prominent citizens, some identified by name, others by occupation — "A Hardware Merchant," "A Municipal Officer," "A Union Depot Policeman." In these chatty paragraphs, the speakers were free to discuss nearly any conceivable topic and did so in often highly literate English. Though many of their discussions might strike us today as composed of garrulous banalities, some of them voice historically interesting points of view, and some few that were intended to amuse savor slightly even yet of their original humor. Readers of the 1880s and 1890s must have found comments like these stimulating, informative, and funny:

> *Prof. H. J. Stout.* The education of young ladies is being revolutionized. Many families of high social standing are beginning to teach their daughters practical book-keeping and business methods, instead of such accomplishments as painting and music. The proportion of young ladies who are able to earn their own livelihood has greatly increased in the last ten years. Nowadays it is a common thing to see young women occupying important clerical positions in large business houses, and they do their work as well as men. Why, it scarcely pays a young man now to learn stenography or book-keeping, for young women are invading that territory and driving men to other pursuits. Look about in St. Louis and you will be surprised to learn how many young ladies are acting as private secretaries, clerks, accountants and stenographers. The young men are surely but slowly being driven into sterner fields of labor, and in a few years more, if women advance in the same ratio as in the past decade, there will be no male clerks behind the counters. Young men will have to adopt trades and professions that by nature are unfitted for the employment of women. But it is all for the best;

clerical work is feminine in its character, and vigorous, strong-minded men will not consent to sell neckties or keep a set of books for a livelihood. Such work belongs to the rising generation of women. The slender, pale-faced young man, whose white soft hands are never soiled with manly labor, will have to seek fresh pastures in the near future, for, as the practical education of women advances it means that they will become strong competitors of men in all indoor work where mental cleverness and physical dexterity are required. The practical education of women will give them strength and independence; it will enable many women to relieve family distresses by contributing to family support, and make wives the invaluable counselors and assistants of their husbands.

[*8 January 1888, p. 6*]

I. N. Joyce. The bouncer is a necessary adjunct of modern civilization, for wherever there are large assemblages periodically gathered the bouncer is as necessary as the proprietor. His name is derived from his peculiar method of performing the functions of his office. Whomsoever the good bouncer ejects goes out largely in the air, and touches the ground only at long intervals. He is the terror of the free-lunch fiend, who presumes upon the theory that free lunches are free. The moment the fiend enters a free-lunch bar-room the bouncer sizes him up, and the next moment the fiend is unceremoniously seized by the nape of the neck and whatever slack of his apparel is most available, and literally bounced along until he reaches the sidewalk. In many saloons the bouncer combines his vocation with other duties. He may be a barkeeper or a waiter, but in halls where beer and music flow together it is becoming necessary to employ a bouncer to do nothing but bounce.

[*8 January 1888, p. 6*]

N. P. Brown. The doctors and electricians say there is no probability of a rheumatic receiving benefit from riding in the electric cars, but, in spite of the doctors and electricians, there are dozens of men who have been materially helped by going to and from their business in the motors. There is a down-town clerk who every winter is laid up, sometimes for weeks at a time, with rheumatism of the lower limbs. It usually begins in October, but this fall, having an idea that the electric cars would do him good, he began riding in them, spending as much time as he could spare in the evening, riding to the end of the line and back, and thus far he has not had a touch of his old trouble, and others can testify to the good that has been done them in the same way. They all say they can feel no current, but in some manner they have been helped, and that is enough for them to know, without bothering to find out how the thing was done.

[*7 December 1890, p. 25*]

"About Old People" and "Local Gossip" preceded "Heard in the Corridors" by several years and probably gave McCullagh the idea for the latter feature. It had long been a practice of newspapers to print the names of out-of-town guests who were visiting local residents or staying at the main hostelries. In the *Globe-Democrat* such lists, called "Personal Mention," "Local Personals," or "Visitors at the Hotels," usually gave only the guest's name and hometown, occasionally his reason for being in St. Louis and his future plans:

A. GAGE, Detroit, is stopping at the Planters'.
W. R. GOULD and wife, Worcester, Mass., are at the Lindell.
MR. P. C. MURRAY, traveling representative of the Dubuque *Daily Evening Telegraph,* who has been at the Southern for the past day or two, contemplates an extended trip through the Southwest.

[*25 February 1883, p. 8*]

Applying his group interview technique to such raw data, McCullagh assigned reporters to gather, from out-of-towners or lobby habitués, comments which would go into a column of three to eight paragraphs, each from one hundred to five hundred words long. "Corridors" appeared first on December 4, 1890, and ran daily (but not on Sunday) for six or seven years thereafter.[2]

In the period before Dreiser arrived, most "Corridors" paragraphs sound, in their plain matter-of-factness, like the faithfully transcribed remarks of actual guests. The locales most favored for these interviews were three leading St. Louis hotels—the Southern, the Laclede, and the Lindell. (The Planters', probably the city's most famous caravansary, was then rebuilding and hence is not mentioned during Dreiser's months with the paper.) Since St. Louis was by this time one of the nation's great commercial hubs, visitors who were interviewed might hail from anywhere—even abroad. "Corridors" reporters seem to have preferred talkative types who could be relied on to supply usable copy—traveling salesmen, small-town politicoes, glib show people, loquacious Southern colonels, anyone who could come up with some mild drollery, tall tale, or yarn, or who was willing to express an opinion on a timely question. More than likely, for these individuals, to be quoted by the great *Globe-Democrat* was a thing to brag about to the folks back home.

As with "Local Gossip" almost any subject could serve as grist. Whatever interested the guest himself, within the bounds of decorum, was acceptable—current events, politics, eccentric characters, incidents funny or sad, etc., etc. The paragraphs were, of course, intended to be read on the run, to provide only a moment's diversion, perhaps with a little food for thought. Occasionally a genuinely humorous or compelling anecdote is found, but usually the severe space limitations do not allow much plot and character development. Since the column's demand for copy was insatiable, it was apparently not unheard of for reporters in a pinch to invent comments and assign them to make-believe guests.

Maintaining the daily supply of "Corridors" material required imaginative reporters of a literary bent. Hence in early November 1892 when Dreiser began work, he was quickly assigned to help out because he had already shown he could do that kind of writing. Indeed, his skill at it had played a large part in winning him a berth on this paper.

Dreiser's brief, abortive newspaper career had begun in Chicago the preceding June, two months before his twenty-first birthday.[3] (It was to end dismally in New York City in March 1895 when he was twenty-three, but that is a story for elsewhere.) His entry into this field had been preceded by an intellectually stimulating if socially embarrassing year at Indiana University (1889–90), which had convinced him that if he were to rise in the world he would have to do it in a more practical way than going to college—what that might be, exactly, he did not know.

Back in Chicago, where his family then lived, he worked at a number of lowly jobs. He was a real estate agent, then a driver of laundry wagons, then an installment collector for firms that sold cheap furnishings to the poor. For none of this was he paid very much, but his work immersed him daily in the colorful, turbulent street life of Chicago, and he soon began to feel an urge to describe that motley scene.

For two or three years now he had been a reader of "Sharps and Flats," Eugene Field's column in the *Daily News*. He admired its highly polished, frequently ironic comments on Chicago life and "seethed to express" himself in a similar way (*Newspaper Days,* p. 3). Aspiring to become a columnist like Field or his colleagues Brand Whitlock, George Ade, and Finley Peter Dunne, he began to practice writing descriptions of events witnessed during the day—fires, accidents, shootings, fights—and, when he judged that his versions were at least as good as those that got printed, he made the rounds of all the best newspapers, looking for a job. But he quickly found that their editors had no place for a greenhorn, so he decided to lay siege to the city's smallest and poorest journal, the *Daily Globe,* figuring that it would not be so particular about whom it hired.

The short-lived *Globe* (1887–93) was indeed a shabby operation. A morning daily and Sunday paper that ran to an average of eight pages an issue, poorly printed and crudely illustrated, it was the property of one Michael Cassius McDonald, a rich out-of-office Democratic politician, gambler, saloon keeper, and bawdyhouse proprietor, who published it solely to tout his own interests and blast those of his Republican foes.[4]

Here Dreiser would appear every day, hoping for a chance to show what he could do, only to be told there was nothing at the moment but that something might turn up soon. His doggedness finally paid off when he was taken on temporarily to help cover the June 1892 Democratic National Convention. By pure luck he got a tip that the party powers were secretly planning to hand the nomination to Grover Cleveland. With this advance information on the biggest story of the Convention, the *Globe* — "too poor to belong to the general news service" — was enabled, if not exactly to scoop its rivals, at least to keep abreast of them (*Newspaper Days,* p. 58).

His reward was a full-time job at fifteen dollars a week. Through the rest of the summer he gained a few of the skills essential to a newsman, in no small part through the kindly offices of John Maxwell, the paper's copy editor, who had taken a liking to the young cub. Under Maxwell's tutelage he developed a knack for ferreting out the newsworthy and writing the sort of feature stories that 1890s readers enjoyed.

Sometime that summer, probably in late July, the *Globe* acquired a new city editor who was to influence Dreiser's journalistic career profoundly. John T. McEnnis, once a respected St. Louis reporter now far gone into drink, sought to infuse the *Globe* with some of the verve and variety of his old paper, the *Globe-Democrat.* (One feature he introduced was an infrequent column of hotel interviews modeled on "Heard in the Corridors.")

Sensing Dreiser's gifts, McEnnis urged him to find work with a better newspaper that could give him more opportunity to grow. Naturally, he talked up the *Globe-Democrat,* stressing that its famed editor liked to develop and reward young talent.

Then, in early autumn, Dreiser was assigned to expose some crooked auction shops that, owing to the benign indifference of the chief of police, were brazenly fleecing naive newcomers to the city. The *Globe*'s true object, of course, was to embarrass the Republican administration, but for Dreiser it was a chance to do an impressive job of investigative reporting. He was working at this task in mid-October when the *Globe-Democrat* sent its Washington correspondent, an old friend of McEnnis's, to Chicago to cover the elaborate formal dedication of the Columbian Exposition, scheduled to open the following spring. Praising Dreiser for his auction-shop exposés, McEnnis urged his friend to let him handle part of this assignment so that McCullagh might see what a promising lad he was and be persuaded to give him a place. The upshot was that Dreiser was given "some easy gossip writing to do," and shortly thereafter McCullagh did offer him a job at twenty dollars a week (*Newspaper Days,* p. 82).

The "easy gossip writing" which opened the door to the *Globe-Democrat* was called "Gossip of Chicago's Big Show," a four-installment mélange of anecdotes, tall tales, and reflections on the Fair, supposedly gathered from people in town for the dedication, one of those mass-interview features so favored by McCullagh. Probably McEnnis had briefed Dreiser on how such assignments were sometimes carried off by the *Globe-Democrat* staff, for, while most of the comments he turned in were apparently made by real people, some are obviously his own inventions. Perhaps in composing the latter he sought to emulate Field's "Sharps and Flats," which he still read faithfully, finding that its commentary on local life moved him "as nothing hitherto had" (*Newspaper Days,* p. 1).

Once in St. Louis, then, it was only natural that Dreiser be assigned to provide copy for "Corridors" in addition to his other reportorial tasks. He continued to do so until April 30th, when he abruptly resigned from the paper in deep embarrassment over having faked some reviews of shows that, unknown to him, had not come to town when they were supposed to, a blunder by which he inadvertently exposed the great McCullagh himself to the sharp ridicule of rival papers.

Certain remarks in Dreiser's autobiography *Newspaper Days* would lead one to believe that during his five months with the *Globe-Democrat* he was solely responsible for "Corridors," but such a large number of paragraphs appeared over those months that it seems unlikely that he was the only contributor. Diligent and productive though he was, it is hardly conceivable that he could handle all his multifarious reportorial duties and still grind out so much copy day after day. Yet the fact that with his departure the column began to be printed only sporadically and did not appear at all from June through November argues that, if he was not the sole contributor, he must certainly have been the principal one. While only 150 of the 828 "Corridors" paragraphs published from 31 October 1892 through 2 May 1893 can be identified as Dreiser's, a great many of the remaining 678 must be his too, even though we cannot be sure which ones they are.

In *Newspaper Days* Dreiser asserts that when he came to the *Globe-Democrat* those reporters who had been providing copy for "Corridors" had pretty well run out of ideas. A review of the columns printed during the ten months prior to his arrival does not entirely bear him out in this, but it is undeniable that once he joined the staff more fanciful and imaginative paragraphs began to appear. The editors must have welcomed a reporter who could provide abundant fresh material. Dreiser himself was delighted with the chance to exercise his powers of imagination, so much so that twenty-five years later his memory of the zest with which he had approached this task was still vivid.

> I discovered that it gave free rein to my wildest imaginings which was exactly what I wanted. I could write any sort of story I pleased, romantic, realistic or lunatic, and credit it to some imaginary guest at one of the hotels, and if it was not too improbable it was passed without comment. . . . I went forth to get names of personages stopping at the hotels. I inquired for celebrities. As a rule, the clerks could give me no information or were indifferent, and seemed to take very little interest in having the hotel advertised. I returned and racked my brain, decided that I could manufacture names as well as stories, and forthwith scribbled six marvels, attaching such names as came into my mind. The next day these were all duly published and I was told to do the column regularly as well as my regular assignments. My asinine ebullience had won me a new task without any increase in pay. (*Newspaper Days,* p. 134)

Writing with apparent ease for an indulgent copy editor and a not overly critical audience, Dreiser spun off paragraph after paragraph on a host of topics. Exercising his newfound gift for story-telling, he learned to express himself with speed and facility. Writing became a natural act for him.

How many of his paragraphs record the remarks of actual people can never be determined. At least some of them must, even though no speaker he names ever appears in the listings of hotel guests in the *Globe-Democrat.* Quite certainly, those paragraphs ascribed to friends or family members were made up. Investigation even reveals that a few others (see Nos. 9, 53, and 62) were simply lifted from printed sources: magazines, newspapers, or standard reference works. Whatever their source, however, they all show the writer's shaping hand, for Dreiser was obliged to make them concise, coherent, and interesting. In doing so he got valuable practice in delineating character, narrating a story, and developing an argument.

His topics are richly varied: unforgettable experiences, eerie and supernatural phenomena, narrow escapes, catastrophes, luck, literature, music, strange folks and folkways, words and their curious ways, money and jewels, plants and animals, birds and fish, new scientific discoveries, memorable personalities, the social importance of new clothes, the strange workings of the mind. Some of the paragraphs are mood pieces, reflective and touched with poetic melancholy, a favorite subject being lonely neglected graveyards. Some were probably inspired by discussions carried on within the bohemian circle Dreiser belonged to in St. Louis. Some, like Nos. 22 and 111, express points of view to which he surely must have felt unsympathetic but which he still found interesting or provocative enough to air in the column. Not a few can now be seen to derive from personal experiences that he described later in his several autobiographies. Indeed, it is not too much to say that in these slight compositions Dreiser discovered how to transmute biography into fiction, a faculty which would become the essence of his novelistic art.

Taken altogether they constitute his first significant body of creative work. They anticipate not only the more mature critical reflections which, a few years later, as editor of *Ev'ry Month,* he would publish under the pseudonym of "The Prophet," but also such characteristic motifs, sounded still later in his novels, as the inherent inequality of men, the function of instinct in behavior, the role of luck in achieving success, the all-importance of money in American life, the saintliness of the loving mother, the nature of literature, and the character of the artist-writer.[5]

Of course, it must be acknowledged that these ephemeral writings have only slight value as literature. In their own right, little more can be claimed for them than a certain quaint period charm. If Dreiser had not written them, they would today merit the attention only of those who delight in the curious and the obscure. Furthermore, to the question of what promise they give of the magnitude of Dreiser's future work, one must candidly reply, very little. A sympathetic reader of the 1890s might have seen talent in them but could not have confidently predicted a significant literary career for whoever wrote them.

But with hindsight we recognize the serious young writer beginning to sense his powers, exercising his storytelling gift, expressing a far-ranging curiosity about people and the world, and responding to nature and the human condition with the feelings of a poet. Not much more can be claimed for the juvenilia of any great writer.

NOTES

1. Information about McCullagh has been obtained from microfilm files of the *St. Louis Globe-Democrat* from 1880 through 1895, from Charles C. Clayton's *Little Mack: Joseph B. McCullagh of the St. Louis Globe-Democrat* (Carbondale: So. Illinois UP, 1969) and from Jim Allee Hart's *A History of the St. Louis Globe-Democrat* (Columbia: U of Missouri P, 1961).

2. It was always printed in the first left-hand column, sometimes running over into the second, of pages 5 and 7, but never on the editorial page as Dreiser mistakenly remembered in *Newspaper Days*.

3. Information about Dreiser's newspaper career has been obtained from his autobiographies *Dawn* (New York: Horace Liveright, 1931) and *A Book About Myself* [*Newspaper Days*] (New York: Boni and Liveright, 1922). *Newspaper Days* was Dreiser's preferred title and the one under which the book was reissued in 1931. The complete manuscript versions of these books, which are in the Dreiser Collection of the University of Pennsylvania, have also been consulted. They reveal nothing further about Dreiser's work on "Heard in the Corridors" than is to be found in the published versions.

4. Dreiser mistakenly gives McDonald's name as John B. Mac-Donald (*Newspaper Days,* p. 79). The correct name is authenticated in Lloyd Wendt and Herman Kogan's *Lords of the Levee* (Indianapolis: Bobbs-Merrill, 1943), p. 27.

5. A large number of representative "Prophet" essays have been reprinted in *Theodore Dreiser: A Selection of Uncollected Prose,* ed. Donald Pizer (Detroit: Wayne State UP, 1977), pp. 36–116.

Theodore Dreiser's "Heard in the Corridors"
Articles and Related Writings

CHICAGO DAILY GLOBE

"About the Hotels"

CHICAGO DAILY GLOBE

DREISER'S first hotel interviews, Nos. 1–4, were written while he was a reporter for the *Chicago Daily Globe,* the first with the heading "Around the Hotels" and the next three with the heading "About the Hotels." They were probably produced at the behest of John T. McEnnis, the city editor, who had formerly been on the staff of the *St. Louis Globe-Democrat,* where he would have been quite familiar with this type of writing.

No. 1.

Thomas E. Garvin, of Evansville, Ind., is in the city at present and yesterday spoke of the political outlook in Indiana and the state World's Fair appropriation. Mr. Garvin said:

"From many indications any one can easily see Indiana is soundly democratic. There is at present less noise and brass band enthusiasm than in any previous campaign. The people of the state are thinking, they are not yelling. All the political vituperation that could be heaped upon the two candidates has been heaped in the two previous campaigns and for once in the history of campaigns the leaders are compelled to discuss facts.

"The farmers of the state have formed their opinions of the situation so that there is little to be gained by stump speaking in our state. Only the leaders, men of note, are now able to draw any kind of a crowd out to listen. Aside from all this we have the result of state and county ballots taken under the Australian law, and they have shown that, political trickery aside, Indiana is democratic.

"Indiana's population is fairly educated. Newspapers are widely read. A canvass of the state shows that democratic and low tariff journals have a larger circulation in the state than any others. Some local issues are now up that in any but a presidential campaign might hurt the party. As it stands the administration for Mr. Cleveland overshadows any petty difficulties at present. The World's Fair is of vast interest to Indiana, and not for any especial exhibit that the state can make but for the knowledge it will bring to our people who visit Chicago. We have appropriated $75,000 and that will be increased to $250,000 this fall. We have nothing especially superior to Illinois or Ohio to exhibit. The state is merely their equal. Such as we have will be displayed to the best advantage, I assure you."

Mr. Garvin will remain in the city until the 25th or 26th to look over the city and visit the Fair grounds.

[17 October 1892, p. 2, col. 5]

No. 2.

There is no place like southern Indiana for graveyards," said William Yakey, of Bloomfield, Indiana, who is stopping at the Auditorium. "Now, that section including Green, Monroe, Brown and Sullivan counties is a wonderland to traverse. It looks as though the old settlers of fifty years ago wanted, each one, to have a graveyard of his own. Every mile or two, often far from any roadway, totally inaccessible to wagons, without laying waste the fences, you come upon little rock walled or rail bound enclosures containing the dead of one family. Father, mother and several children lie there, and none others.

"These places have long been forsaken and forgotten. Weeds flourish in profusion and hide the wind and rain stained tombstones from view. Often with a companion I have entered one of those little enclosures, trampled and tore out the weeds and righted the five or six headstones that had fallen and buried even the inscribed virtues of the dead into the wormy earth.

"These people had no country church yard. No preacher except the visiting parson who came monthly on horseback. They had no funeral · in the present sense of the word. Plain wooden boxes were used for coffins and often the sturdy youth of the family made the coffin for the dead parent or relative. These little spots were dear to those families. One can see that by the loving little

inscriptions and decorations. When they were all dead no one remained to care for them and they fell·into decay and ruin.

"They are lonesome sights, those little groups of white pillars. In the winter when the trees are bare and the grass dead, I have seen flocks of crows coming and circling about the little clump of trees that usually cluster about those places. The bitter wind moans through the crackling branches and those crows wheel about and caw and croak until the world seems truly a place of sorrow and death."

[*29 October 1892, p. 2, cols. 4–5*]

No. 3.

There's a light house on the rock reef that lies out in the ocean from my old town," said A. P. Corwaith, of Pennrock, Maine, "and they tell a queer story of it. Within the last ten years they have had three keepers for it, and all have left for some reason or other. It was about ten years ago that old Uncle Billy Curtis died there. He had been keeper for twenty-five long years, and Uncle Billy would climb the winding flight of stairs toward night and light the beacon that pointed out the position of the dangerous ledge.

"I can see that old tower yet with its yellow light shining through the bleak storms of night and blinking through the driven snows of winter. Old Billy was faithful though, and the shadows never fell without the light replacing in a measure their absence.

"One night about the time I speak of an awful storm came up. Oh! it just howled around my home. It was bleak and rainy, and the wind was furious. It was not long after dark until every one in the village was talking of a certain fact. Uncle Billy's light was not burning. Nothing could be done, however. There was not one in Pennrock who would venture to row out and light the beacon. It remained that way for the night and the next day the storm passed over. Then a party rowed out and investigated the cause. There was cause enough, I assure you; old Uncle Billy was dead. He had dropped from heart disease, old age, or something, but at any rate he was no more. I left there not long after and came west to Denver. I have just been home now to visit, and what I have to tell that is curious is how Uncle Billy's death has become a legend.

"Some of those old fish wives relate the story now with marvellous elongation. They have every detail of Billy's dying looks and thoughts. They say now that on the night of his death he climbed to the tower, lighted the lamp and came down again. All the while this terrible storm was raging. He was suddenly taken ill and just as he expired the light went out in the tower. They saw it with their own eyes. Now, of course, they claim the tower is haunted, and that Billy's ghost nightly climbs the tower stairs with a tramp, tramp, tramp, to light the lamp. A sturdy young German has the job now, and he cares more for pork sausage than he does for ghosts, so I guess Billy will not bother him.

"It is queer, though, how these fantastic tales arise over the graves of the hardest facts. It only requires time, and that is all. I know the facts in this instance, and that is why it seems queer."

[*29 October 1892, p. 2, cols. 4–5*]

No. 4.

I was lost in a cave once," said R. L. Jeffery, who is stopping at the Wellington. "It was in 1883, down in Kentucky, and the cave was known as 'Slamer's hole.' I was under the impression that I knew that cave to perfection. It was not large and I often ventured into it alone with a torch and a string tied to the entrance. I was raised within six miles of it, and I had been in it upwards of twenty times before this occasion.

"One bright morning a friend came over and wanted me to accompany him on a visit to the cave. I don't think that up to this time I ever refused an invitation to go to Slamer's hole. Well, we set out with two torches and several balls of sheep twine measuring about 800 feet. The entrance was simply a hole in the side of a hill, covered with brush and overhanging limbs, and a log lay just in front, obscuring it from view. We struck out through the fields with our lunches and torches and at last came to the entrance and slipped in.

"For about fifty feet it was a narrow passage, rock bound, that opened into the first large chamber. We followed the various passages, unwinding the twine and finally came to the end of the string. My partner was for turning back, but the passage that we were in looked straight and narrow and I proposed that we set up a stone, tie the string and go to the end. Well we did. The passage was stopped about fifty feet ahead, a wall of jagged rocks ascending from there perpendicularly. I had never been farther than this. Hand over hand we ascended to the top ledge. At the top was a small mouth entering into a larger chamber. We looked through, viewed the entrance so that we might know it again, then drew ourselves through. The room was immense. Down in the distance our torch fires were reflected in the underground waters of a stream. We were awe struck and stood listening to the constant drip, drip, drip of falling water.

"My friend climbed down and stood on the shore of that dark stream, a veritable Pluto's realm it was. Then I thought of the entrance. I turned to view it just to regain a feeling of security. It was not there. I lowered my torch and walked to and fro, but could not see it. I became numb with fear. An indefinite dread, a something horrible tugged at my nerves until I hallooed in sheer terror the name of my companion—Hall. It was the sound of my voice that brought him running to my side. We both looked again. It was not to be seen. Then we stopped for a moment. Vague thoughts of ghosts and demons, of starving and of wandering mad in that infinite blackness filled me with horrors. For a moment I was almost demented. We dropped on our knees and began a crawling search. There were several large outlets, but we knew they led us elsewhere than out.

"The last move was the correct one. We had crawled in, we might crawl out. Our mistake was plain. The mouth we entered through was overhung by a flat rock. We had not noticed that. When we stood up on the inside the mouth was invisible. How we stumbled, hurried, fell along that passageway and out into the sunlight I can not describe.

"At last the daylight streamed like electricity through the aperture, the entrance. When we came out it was afternoon. The sun was low. Trees, grass and sunlight never looked so fair. A breeze never felt so sweet and cool before. We lay down on that grassy hillside and rested. I was thankful and at peace then, but I never again visited 'Slamer's' or any other cave since."

[*29 October 1892, p. 2, cols. 4–5*]

St. Louis Globe-Democrat

"Gossip of Chicago's Big Show"

St. Louis Globe-Democrat

FROM October 21 through 24 of 1892 under the title "Gossip of Chicago's Big Show," the *St. Louis Globe-Democrat* ran four multicolumn groups of interviews with people attending the dedicatory ceremonies of the Columbian Exposition. Dreiser was hired temporarily to supply all or most of the copy for these features. Nos. 5–18 are excerpted to illustrate the skill and variety of his writing in this vein.

No. 5.

Do you believe in luck?" Gov. Merriam, of Minnesota, was asked. "To a certain extent, yes. I think I have had my share, don't you?" he replied laughing. "I'll tell you of one piece of luck that happened to me," he continued. "In the early days of Northwestern emigration I was fortunate enough to obtain a pre-emption and homestead claim adjoining in the eastern part of the State. When I proved up upon my pre-emption claim I determined to move my little log shanty over on to the homestead, but that was easier said than done at that time. Horses were scarce, and human assistance even more so. I saw but one way out of it—to pull down the modest dwelling, haul the lumber over to the other farm and rebuild. I sat in the shanty one night after a hard day's plowing thinking over plans for the removal, when suddenly there came an awful gust of wind, followed by a regular Western cyclone, and I felt the building being lifted bodily in the air. My head struck against the wall and I was rendered unconscious. When I came to myself I went outside, and was thunderstruck to find that the shanty had been lifted by the elements over to my homestead claim. How was that for luck?"

[*21 October 1892, p. 6, col. 5*]

No. 6.

A queer incident you want, eh?" said Col. Elbrook, of Denton, Ind.; "something that will interest and surprise readers. Here is one. Back in 1837 my father, who then lived near Corydon, the old State capital of Indiana, decided to sell out and move farther north, because he liked Northern Indiana better. He succeeded in selling sixty acres of his land there, but another sixty he could not get rid of. He placed it in the care of a neighbor, packed up his necessary household utensils in a large wagon, and with mother and the three young boys started to drive about 200 miles north. I ought to say that he was not alone. Two other farmers were of the party, altogether having four wagons. Father had been up near what is now known as Silver Lake, Ind., and had traded with some Indians for sixty acres of land. I won't describe the Silver Lake, or his farm, or the Indians, but my point is relative to the three boys, Jake, George, Severius. I have heard my father tell it like this: 'My boys were fine lads; Jake was 11 years old. George was 7 and Severius was 5. They were strong, healthy lads, but I felt six months before they died that they were going to die. I told my wife so. One evening before we left Corydon—about a month before—I was splitting wood for the supper fire. It was still early in the spring and the nights were damp and misty. From the wood-pile, near the kitchen door, you could look over a field of stumps down into a swamp. I stopped in my work as a man will do occasionally and looked out over the field. Down in that swamp I saw three lights moving about over the fog. I watched them for a minute and they seemed to be coming toward me. I waited, and they were pale, like alcohol burns, and about the size of a medium candle flame. They hurried by through the field and over the rail fence that we had around the house. They passed within 10 feet of me and went out as they reached the house. I pondered over that and told my wife of it, but she laughed it away. I had almost forgotten the incident when one night while we were on the road

north, I saw three similar lights—will-'o-the-wisps—come through an open space near the road and disappear in the woods beyond. A month afterwards, it was the last of June, 1837, I was sitting outside the kitchen door grinding coffee for supper, with a little iron hand mill. It was fairly light still, but anyhow I saw those three lights again. They came from a heavy patch of woods about 200 yards from the door. I felt just as I did that night splitting wood down in Corydon. They came past me, and passed into the woods beyond the house. The oldest of my boys, Jake, took sick a month afterward, and died in three weeks. Then George got the fever and died, and little Severius followed last. They died about a month apart. It was very queer, and people say pshaw when I tell it, but I am sure those lights were a token.'

"My father was a very broad man and a prominent citizen. He wasn't much on religion, but he was h--l on justice and well thought of. It may be nonsense, but coming from him, it was certainly a very queer story."

[*21 October 1892, p. 6, col. 6*]

No. 7.

M any people have wondered," said Mr. J. Catesby, of Philadelphia, "why that great and good man, Archbishop Ryan, has not been honored by the Holy See with a Cardinal's cap. I believe I know the reason. Not long ago I had a conversation with Cardinal Gibbons, and he intimated to me that the antagonism displayed by Archbishop Ryan to the advocated plans of Cahensley was objectionable to his Holiness the Pope. If that be true, the majority of American citizens will sympathize with the Archbishop, for the ideas of Cahensley will never find popular favor in this country. To send over German priests with German emigrants — or any other nationality, for that matter — speaking a foreign language is wrong. Such a proceeding would tend to perpetuate foreign tongues in America, and that is antagonistic to the principles laid down in the Declaration of Independence. Archbishop Ryan is right in opposing the Cahensley doctrine, and he is not a man to sacrifice his ideas of what is best for this people for the greatest honors in the gift of the holy executive at Rome."

[*22 October 1892, p. 4, cols. 3–4*]

No. 8.

A new device for plucking strangers has been invented by the keeper of a big Clark street restaurant. He didn't want to frighten regular customers away by raising prices on his bill of fare, and yet felt that it was a shame to be behind boarding house keepers, saloons and hotels in overcharging. Yesterday a bright idea struck him,

and he promptly put it into operation. A waiter gave the snap away. "I've eaten there for six months," said a well-known merchant, "and seldom had cause for complaint. Last night I ordered a sirloin steak, as I had often done before. It was much thinner than usual, but I was not particularly hungry and did not complain. This morning I was served with a still thinner one, and kicked. Then the waiter told me the steaks were all being cut thinner this week because so many strangers were in town, and the boss wanted to get more for meals without driving away the regulars. It's the same way everywhere else. The pies are smaller, so are the pats of butter, and the proprietor has actually run in a lot of new coffee cups that hold considerably less than the old ones."

[*22 October 1892, p. 4, col. 4*]

No. 9.

The name of Breckinridge, in Kentucky, has come to be very closely connected with Presbyterian doctrines. Since any one can remember the Breckinridges, some of them, have been active in Presbyterian General Assemblies. Some of them have not been so closely identified with the doctrines of John Calvin. Gen. John C. Breckinridge, of the United States army, has a theory that this long relationship to the Church has left its physical imprint on the Breckinridge face, and he tells this story to illustrate his point: Not long ago he stood on the street of a mining camp in the West. A gentleman who was about to pass stopped, turned and looked closely at him. Rather stiffly the General said, "Well, sir?" Without another word the stranger asked: "What is the chief end of man?" "My memory," says Gen. Breckinridge, in telling the incident, "went backward for at least forty years, to the time when I had last seen the shorter catechism. 'Man's chief end,' I replied, 'is to glorify God and enjoy him forever.' 'I knew you were a Presbyterian,' said the stranger. 'I can tell a Presbyterian as far as I can see him.' "

[*22 October 1892, p. 4, col. 4*]

No. 10.

It was on State street, near Washington, in front of the Memorial Building viewing stand. An old darky clad in shiny suit and wearing a slouch hat shut off a view of the parade by waving a huge United States flag as the various detachments passed. Finally a gentleman spoke up and said:

"George, we can't see through that flag; put it down."

"Aw do'ant care whethah yoah can or not," was the reply. "It's good enough foh me. I'se bohn under dat flag and I'm gwine to wave it."

This satisfied the crowd and the darky kept it up until the colored Knights of Pythias, in all the glories of the rainbow, arrived. Then he jumped out into the street, waved the flag more than before and cheered at the top of his voice. After the darky patriots had passed, he stepped back, rolled up the flag and remarked:

"I'se done my duty, sah."

As long as the Knights were in sight the old darky with the slouch hat looked down the street after them.

And the crowd that once objected to the flag cheered the old man as lustily as any of the celebrities who had passed before.

[*22 October 1892, p. 4, col. 5*]

No. 11.

Senator John M. Palmer reflected yesterday over the story printed in a local paper to the effect that the Illinois Democratic nominee for Governor tried to beat him out of his election for Senator. "If any of Palmer's fool friends believe that story it's all right," said the Senator. "None of my friends will be influenced by it, and if they are they are my friends no longer so it's the same. Everybody has fool friends and John M. Palmer is no exception."

[*23 October 1892, p. 23, col. 1*]

No. 12.

There is only one incident in my life which will forever remain a mystery to me," said Richard Fairchild, a young lawyer of Indianapolis, Ind. "They may talk about the nonsense of telepathy, clairvoyancy and all that kind of thing, but I am won over to a belief that there is something about the mind which is not understood. My father was a railway mail clerk, having a through run from Indianapolis to Philadelphia. The limited made extraordinary fast time through Virginia, going over the mountains and around the great curves at the rate of forty miles per hour. It is in connection with one of these trips that my story has to do. Before I began the practice of law I was a clerk in an insurance office in which there was employed a large number of clerks and typewriters. One day shortly after 11 o'clock in the morning I heard my father call me, or rather I thought I did. In coming in from off his trips he always came straight to see me before going home to mother. This day the train was not due, however, and I was not expecting him, and when I heard my name called in the old familiar manner I turned to greet my father with surprise. He was not in the room, however, and I walked to the door and looked into the hall. He was not there either. I wondered at the occurrence. Something possessed me, a strange feeling of dread, a desire to look farther and find him before I returned to work. With this object in view I started out of the office and down the street toward the depot which he usually traversed in coming to the office. I did not meet him on the way, and the train had not yet arrived. Dissatisfied with the result of my search I returned to the office and inquired if my father had been there. 'You look restless,' said one; 'what's the matter?'

" 'Why, I want to see my father.'

" 'Your father?'

" 'Yes. I heard him call me here in the office, and I thought he was here.'

"The clerks in the office laughed at the idea and told me that I was sick or 'off my base.' The time at which I heard the voice was 11:06 a.m., for I remember glancing at the clock and clearly marking the time. I tried to resume work, but I did not do so successfully. In a little while a message was brought to the office saying that the train on which my father was mail clerk was wrecked while passing around a mountain curve, and that my father had been instantly killed.

"I have thought over that occurrence again and again. I can recall the sound of my father's voice vividly. I think that father, realizing that he and I were supporting mother and sister, and that now I would be left alone to take up the burden, and wishing in his love for mother and sister to impress me with the sense of my responsibility, had spoken my name, and that I heard it. I believe this most firmly, and I am sure the remembrance of his voice has aided me in my duty many times since. The coincidence is strengthened when I tell you that the accident, according to the dispatch and later advices, occurred shortly after 11 o'clock a.m. and that I heard his voice simultaneously."

[*23 October 1892, p. 23, col. 2*]

No. 13.

I do not know of any mechanical or physical phenomenon," said Paul Dresser, the famous author of so many lyrical ballads, "but I can tell you a story of animal devotion that was beautiful to witness, and true. On one of my tours through the country our company stopped at Boise City, Idaho, where we played for three nights. Our engagement ended on Saturday night, and we could not leave town until Sunday night at 10:30. It was a beautiful Sunday that greeted my eyes next morning, and I resolved to take a stroll along one of the roads leading north from the city. After breakfast I set out for a good long walk. About four miles out of the city I came to an old log house, situated far back from the road. Nothing particularly strange about the place caused me to notice it, but I did observe that it looked as though the family had shut up the place and gone to church. It did not look any too prosperous, and I put the owner down as being shiftless. A mile further on I came to a graveyard, a little plot of ground bounded about by bushes and a rail fence. Probably I have a morbid desire for that which

is sad and gloomy, but, at any rate, I always enjoy a stroll alone in a quiet country churchyard. I went along the road toward the entrance, which was a whitewashed wooden turn-stile. I walked about the place looking at some inscriptions on the white stones over the graves of miners long since dead. Over in one corner was a row of graves, some with wooden head pieces, on which were inscribed their virtues or lack of virtues, and some without any mark whatever. On one, a new one, the last of a new row, sat a dog, a brown and white dog, eyeing me in a most forsaken manner. I thought for a moment that some one must be near to whom the dog belonged, but my searching glances revealed no one. I watched the animal for fully ten minutes, then I began to coax him to come to me. My good intentions and kind calls were rewarded with an ominous growl. I grew interested, and thought to inquire of the first person whom I should meet.

"It was about noontide that I turned to go, but I had not walked very far before I met a rough-looking stranger who was carrying in his hand some pieces of meat. 'For the dog,' I thought, and sure enough it was for the dog. The stranger walked to the grave and threw the meat down. He did not wait long to see the dog eat, but turned upon his heel and retraced his steps. I met him and asked what the dog was doing. 'Watching,' said the stranger.

" 'Watching, eh? For whom?' I asked.

" 'That's old Jack Squires lying there,' was the reply. 'He lived a mile up the road here. He died three days ago and they buried him here yesterday. He's had the dog ever since it was a pup, four or five years now, and the dog wants to see Jack again. I can't coax nor drive him away. He's been laying there since yesterday morning and I suppose he'll stay there.'

" 'Jack ain't got no monument,' continued the stranger, 'nor probably won't git one, but he's got that dog and that's a heap more than some.'

"With this the stranger walked away. I inquired after Jack Squires at the hotel that evening. He was only a miner that lived alone, not laying up any wealth, but simply supporting himself and the dog. There was nothing remarkable about the man's history, but I do think that the affection of that dog for him holds an untold tale, touching the deepest springs of affection."

Mr. Dresser is the author of fifty-three songs, the most popular of which were "The Letter That Never Came" and "Since Nellie Went Away."

[*23 October 1892, p. 23, col. 3*]

No. 14.

"The cigarette has its friends as well as enemies," said Dr. McNamara, assistant house physician at the Great Northern Hotel; "but from this time on I will stand arrayed as one of its strongest opponents. I have just come from the room of one of the most horrible deaths I ever saw; and yet the case possessed remarkable medical features. The case was that of a young man of a well-known South Side family, who undoubtedly fell a victim to the cigarette. 'Haemoptysis' is the cause of death returned on the certificate, yet it was not a real bleeding of the lungs, but rather a bleeding of the lips, which caused his death. I was called in on the case two weeks ago and since that time have labored incessantly to prevent death, but outraged nature could not be appeased. I found the young man suffering from a slight hemorrhage of the under lip. A small sore had formed there, on the spot where the cigarette was held between the lips. Drop by drop the blood was slowly dripping from the lip. I first attempted bandages but they were useless. I next cauterized the sore, but that seemed to aggravate it, and the hemorrhage became more violent. Day after day his lifeblood flowed away. I called in brother physicians and every resource known to medical science was used to stop the dreadful extravasation but without effect. This afternoon the patient died, reduced almost to a skeleton. The young man was in the habit of smoking from forty to fifty cigarettes a day. An examination of his blood revealed the fact that the red corpuscles had been reduced 47 per cent, the fluid thus losing its power of coagulation. Inhalation of cigarettes caused this physiological change, and nothing else."

[*24 October 1892, p. 4, col. 5*]

No. 15.

I owe my present trip to Chicago to rats," remarked Harry D. Knowles, a young man from Battle Creek, Mich. "This may appear a remarkable statement, but it is the truth. My uncle, Hiram Knowles, was a crusty old bachelor, worth about $40,000 in farming property. He lived about six miles from Green Corners, St. Clair County, Mich. I had always been more or less a favorite with Uncle Hiram, and it was pretty generally understood that I was to come in for a good share of his money when he passed in. But a little escapade of mine in college which compelled me to retire soured the old gentlemen on me. And, moreover, he began to show an entirely unreasonable affection for a young widow of the neighborhood, and I began to consider my chances up the spout. But fortune sometimes favors the unworthy, as it did me. I knew that Uncle Hiram had made a new will, in which I had reason to believe he had left most of his property to the young woman in question. So when, after a short illness, he unexpectedly died, I had little hope of being remembered. But strangely enough, when the will was found it had been nibbled almost to pieces by rodents. The old gentleman, following his usual eccentric disposition, had hidden the paper on top of an antique wardrobe, where it had furnished food for the hungry rats which haunted the house. The legatee's name had been entirely eaten away, and, as the direct heir, I immediately put in a claim for the property. The affair made great feeling in the neighborhood for a time and the young woman threatened to contest, but my lawyers were able to convince her of the folly of such a course, and I quietly took possession. As I said, I owe my fortune to 'rats,' and you may be sure I will always have a kindly feeling for these generally despised animals."

[*24 October 1892, p. 4, col. 5*]

No. 16.

Here is a land phenomenon which will interest you," said John I. McGreggor, of Clear Creek, Ind. "The land I speak of forms a portion of a farm that I own in that section. The whole territory for miles around, in fact all that section, is undermined with caves, and any amount of holes can be found that lead down into these places. This land in question must cover a large chamber of one of these caves, at least so it would seem. One-fourth of an acre is about the size of the space, and I have fenced it in and put up danger signs. You can walk out into the center of that space and standing in the middle jump up and down, and all of that one-fourth acre will vibrate and quiver to a distance of 200 feet in every direction. Very little exertion is required to start it, and I have seen small boys, certainly not weighing more than 80 pounds, jumping up and down, and then standing still to enjoy the swaying sensation. Nothing ever grows on that spot. Even weeds do not flourish. In the wet springtime it is sometimes covered with a very small growth of very fibrous grass, but this is burnt up by the heat of June and July. I was told by the former owner that when he first took the place he endeavored to plow it. The soil that he turned up did not contain any productive matter, being composed of limestone, small pebbles, etc. In driving the horse to and fro he noticed that the ground swayed, and becoming alarmed at the motion drove his horse off and dropped the matter entirely. He put the fence around the place and I put up the danger signs when I secured the place. The land in the immediate vicinity is fairly productive, yielding moderate crops of wheat, etc. I have traveled somewhat extensively in cave districts and noticed the peculiarities of the climate and soil, but I have never yet come across a similar phenomenon."

[*24 October 1892, p. 4, col. 5*]

No. 17.

I only had a short experience in the South," said Mr. William Clark, formerly Assistant Superintendent of the Wabash Railway system, "but I learned enough to know that the people down there will stand no foolishness from 'mean niggers.' I was a young man at the time and had charge of the Queen and Crescent line at Shreveport, La. I was superintending the loading up of some cotton one day when a big burly negro—a discharged employe of the company—came up and began blustering and interfering with the work. I was a new man in the South and wanted to go slow. The fellow finally became so abusive, however, that I hit him over the head with the butt end of my revolver and laid him out.

"Just then the chief of the police— Hi Rogers—came along and asked what was the matter. I explained the situation, and he inquired, in a surprised tone:

" 'Didn't you kill him?'

"I replied that I didn't want to do anything of that kind.

" 'Why didn't you?' Rogers remarked regretfully. 'Kill him; that's the thing to do.'

" 'Wouldn't I get into trouble?' I inquired.

" 'Trouble! Of course not. Go ahead; kill him,' was Rogers' advice, and he walked away.

"The negro regained his senses shortly and again became obstreperous. I had handed my revolver in the meantime to my assistant, a colored man named Frank. Frank slugged the fellow again and down he went. Mayor Andy Curry happened along about this time, and he also appeared surprised that I had not killed the negro. He earnestly advised me to do so, saying that they had made every arrangement to take care of obstreperous negroes, and that I would be perfectly justified in doing it.

" 'You'll just save us the trouble,' remarked Curry philosophically. 'Don't let him make another pass at you.'

'However, I did not kill the negro, and am glad of it. But it's a bad country for 'sassy niggers,' and they have either got to behave themselves or pass in."

[*24 October 1892, p. 4, col. 6*]

No. 18.

I was on the trail of John L. Sullivan for two years," said Prof. George Siler, the lightweight champion of New York in 1874, who is stopping at the Auditorium. Prof. Siler is the most expert boxer in the United States, an associate of Prof. John Donoven, of the Coney Island Club, and a warm friend of James Corbett, the champion.

"I was rather a hard character in those days, traveling about with the pugilists in New York City, and one night I was in a saloon on the Bowery in company with John L. Sullivan and a large crowd of other sporting gentlemen. It was just after the Sullivan-Ryan fight, and Sullivan having conquered was a little god among the sports of New York and Boston. He was greatly swelled with pride and stood about in most people's way looking belligerent, and citing himself as authority. A question came up for discussion in Murphy's saloon, something about a prize-

fight, and I took one view of the matter, while Sullivan and the entire crowd took another. The argument had not gone very far when John L. exclaimed: 'What do you know about it, anyhow? I know what I'm talking about. Ain't I the champion.' I said: 'It doesn't make any difference whether you're the champion or not, you're wrong. You don't know anything.' 'Shut up,' yelled Sullivan. 'You're a blanked liar, anyhow.'

"He had no sooner called me the name than I whirled about and struck him in the mouth. The gang grabbed me, and while I was endeavoring to tear loose I received an awful blow in the eye that laid me out on the floor. By the time I picked myself up my eye was swollen shut and perfectly black. I looked about on the crowd with the other eye and asked some of the gang, 'Who hit me?' No one would say. I thought it was Sullivan, but I was not certain, and I wanted to be sure. Finally I said, 'Well I'll be back here in a minute,' and I hurried down to a saloon kept by a friend of mine and borrowed a revolver. Then I went back to Murphy's. When I came in the saloon was empty. I asked the barkeeper where they had gone, but he could not tell me and I walked out. I canvassed every saloon, and I knew most of them in those days, where Sullivan and the rest of the crowd were liable to go, but at the various places they had not been seen. After fruitless search I went home, resolved to take the first opportunity for getting even. Two days later there was an entertainment given at one of the gardens. I knew that every sport in town would be there and I thought that Sullivan would be there also. About 7 o'clock in the evening I entered the place and strolled along one of the side corridors toward the stage. At the end of the corridor were gathered the entire crowd that was with me the night I was struck in the eye. Only Sullivan was absent. I walked up to the gang and asked each of them separately, 'Who struck me?' They all told me that no one had struck me; that I was drunk, and that in my struggles to release myself I had slipped and fallen on my face. In this manner they accounted for my swollen eye. I began almost to believe them — in fact, to think that I did not know what I was doing at the time, and that they were telling me the truth. Well, after that I dropped the matter and did not think anything more of it. A year or so afterwards I was touring the country, giving exhibitions of fistic skill, when one evening after the performance I met one of that old original gang that was in the saloon that night. I invited him to come and have lunch with me, and while we were eating and talking over old times, he remarked, 'Say, do you remember the night Sullivan hit you in the eye?' I said 'Yes, did he? I thought so.' Then he told me all about it — how the crowd was certain that I meant to get even, and how they warned John L. to keep out of my way. They had made it up between them to tell me that no one had struck me and so to hush the matter up. By that time my anger had passed away and I did not endeavor to locate John L. very hard. My tour led around later on in the season to this city. I was knocking about one evening enjoying myself when I strolled into a saloon down on Fourth avenue. I walked in and looked about and there I saw Sullivan at one of the tables reading a paper. I walked over to him and said: 'Hello, Sullivan, I suppose you remember me?' He looked at me for a few moments and then exclaimed: 'Why, it's Siler. Hello, old fellow, come, have a drink. Shake, by ----, I'm glad to see you.' He seemed so friendly and desirous of keeping peace that I refrained from raking up the old difference and I drank with him in friendship. I'm sure he remembered the old trouble and felt anxious to allay the difference. So I looked for him two years and then dropped it after all."

[*24 October 1892, p. 4, col. 7*]

St. Louis Globe-Democrat

"Heard in the Corridors"

St. Louis Globe-Democrat

DREISER began writing "Heard in the Corridors" interviews, real and fictional, almost immediately upon joining the *Globe-Democrat* in early November 1892 and continued contributing them regularly until his abrupt departure from the paper late the following April. The selection which follows, Nos. 19-168, consists of all the paragraphs unquestionably by him, together with a number showing characteristics that make his authorship of them highly probable.

No. 19.

I had a very embarrassing adventure in Chicago during the Democratic Convention," said John W. Phelps, now at the Laclede. "I was coming down State street in a pouring rain and with my umbrella held before rather than above me. I turned a corner suddenly and ran square against a little man who was making tracks in the opposite direction. My new silk umbrella was ruined by the collision and the little man's tall tile went rolling into the gutter and began to float downstream. He lost his temper and gave me to understand that I was very far from being the wisest man on earth. In short he told me very pointedly that I was a fool. I was in no very good humor myself, and when that dapper little dude jumped onto me I used language that would not adorn a Sunday-school book. 'Pick up my hat, sir,' he commanded in piping tones, as he danced about in the storm. That was the last straw. I stood my shattered umbrella up in a doorway and advanced on the enemy. 'What, sir! would you strike a woman?' the little fellow piped out. Then I tumbled. It was Dr. Mary Walker. I fished her silk tile out of the gutter, handed it to her with my best bow, murmured a lame apology and took a sneak."

[*3 November 1892, p. 7, no. 1*]

No. 20.

No, I am not exactly a Buddhist, but I do believe a portion of the doctrine taught by Gautama," said Robert Senteny to the little coterie of travelers that were discussing theology in the rotunda of the Lindell. "I believe that I have lived in this world before. I not only believe it, but I know it as well as it is possible for the human mind to know anything. I retain some shadowy memories of a former life—of several former lives, in fact. I have a faint recollection of having been a farmer in the land where the tools were very primitive, and the people wore a dress entirely unknown to any modern nation. I believe that I was a Greek soldier, and present at the battle of Marathon. In fact, I think I was killed there, almost torn to pieces. I remember having seen William of Orange crowned King of England. These memories are so shadowy that they might be mere vagaries of the mind and count for nothing, but I have much stronger proof of a previous existence. I can pick out the places where I lived before. I recognize them the moment I see them, and can tell what changes have occurred in the landscape. I visited the Tower of London some years ago. I had never seen a picture of it nor read of it in history, yet I could point out every change that has been made in the old pile since the days of William and Mary. I traveled over England looking for my old home, and I found it. I recognized the landscape at once. A considerable hill had been cut down to fill a marsh. No one living there knew the hill had ever existed, but I knew it, and a consultation of old records proved it. I visited Greece. I knew that at some period I had lived there, and died there. I found nothing familiar until I reached the plain of Marathon. It was familiar to me as the face of my wife. I needed no guide to point out the position of the armies or the slight changes which have occurred in the topography of the country, for I was an eyewitness of the battle. I have talked with many people who have shadowy recollections of a previous existence, who, like myself, were not well dipped in the River Lethe. If this is my first experience on earth where did I get my knowledge of England during the reign of William of Orange? Where did I learn the topography of the plain of Marathon? How did I know that old hill had been carted away? Why is it that faces that have been dust for centuries are familiar to me as those of my family? There is a bundle of knots for your professors of psychology."

[*3 November 1892, p. 7, no. 5*]

No. 21.

I'll wager the wine there is not a gentleman present who can guess within ten years of my age," said Calvin S. Freeman, who sat talking with some fellow traveling men in the rotunda of the Southern. The guesses ran all the way from 48 to 65. "I am just 34 years old," said Mr. Freeman. "I was born in 1858. I grew old in a day. I have passed through the most terrible ordeal to which a mortal was ever subjected—I was buried alive and lay in the grave, with 6 feet of earth on top of me, for nearly three hours. That was at Edinburgh, Scotland, nearly nine years ago. I was born in that city. At the age of 24 I married a girl who had been my playmate in childhood. A year later I was taken sick and, after an illness of but two days, was pronounced dead, and preparations were made for my burial. I was as conscious as at this moment, but unable to speak or move a muscle. A great weight seemed to lie on my chest and eyelids. All that night and until 10 o'clock next day I lay with a cloth over my face, listening to the preparations for my interment. At that hour I was placed in a coffin, the funeral services were read and I was consigned to the grave. There was no stifling sensation, for I had ceased to breathe, but the black loneliness of those hours haunts me day and night. I felt that I would come out of the trance state before death ensued, would slowly smother to death, and the thought added horror to my situation. I had read of graves being opened where people had been buried alive, and how they had torn their flesh with their nails and turned over in their coffins in a mad struggle for air. I wondered if there was any way by which I could quickly destroy myself when nature asserted its sway. Every hour seemed to me as days. It was Tuesday when I was buried, and I fancied I could hear the Sunday chimes of the church which stood a few yards distant. I wondered who my neighbor was on the right and who on the left, and if they, too, were buried alive. I wondered if there really was such a thing as death, or if I was doomed to lie conscious in that prison forever. Suddenly I felt a muscle twitch. 'It is coming now,' I thought. 'A minute more and I will be struggling for breath.' I felt a faint flutter at the heart. I gave a little gasp and the air seemed freighted with lead. I tried to breathe, but it was like drawing fetid water into my lungs. I had resolved not to move a muscle, to die with my hands folded on my breast, so that if my body was ever taken up my friends would not suspect the awful truth, but I could not lie still. The struggle began, and I fought in my narrow prison house as a man only fights for life. Horrible as it was, I seemed to hear my wife's voice ringing in my ears. It was a cry of agony. I tried to answer it, but could not. A succession of thunder peals shook my prison house. It was the heavy blows of axes breaking open the box which contained the coffin. A moment later I was lying on the churchyard sward in my wife's arms. After my interment she conceived the notion that I had been buried alive, and, to quiet her fears, the grave was opened. I went into the grave a young man, and came out aged, as you see me now."

[*3 November 1892, p. 7, no. 6*]

No. 22.

Some philosopher whose card I have mislaid, once remarked: 'As between men and dogs, give me dogs,' " said Stephen Howe, an old ship captain, as he rolled to a seat in the rotunda of the Lindell. "I have been frequently tempted to indorse the sentiment. When a dog tells me that he is my friend I bank on his statement every time. When a man tells me the same thing I wonder if he is telling the truth. When the man chances to be a woman, I reject it as preposterous. Not one man in a dozen knows what friendship is. Not one woman in a thousand has the slightest conception of its meaning. But the measliest 'yaller' cur that ever skulked in back alleys and picked his living out of garbage barrels understands it. Affection is never wasted on a dog. It is always repaid with compound interest. Once a friend, always a friend—that's a dog. Friendly to-day, enemy to-morrow—that's a man. Friend this minute, backbiting and selling you out the next—that's a woman. One of the most touching incidents of a dog's devotion that ever came under my observation occurred during my last voyage around the Horn in 1878. The first mate was named Spiller. He had a bull-terrier which he had raised from a pup, and which, for several years, had been his constant companion. Bige—that was the dog's name—had been twice around the world with his master, had survived two shipwrecks and only needed hands to become an able seaman. During the voyage I spoke of, Spiller was taken ill and lay for many days unconscious. During all that time Bige never left his master's bedside. He hung about him, moaning like a child. He realized his master's danger, and could hardly be persuaded to take food or drink. Finally Spiller became delirious. He raved and swore, and Bige howled as though his heart would break. Frequently in his delirium Spiller would call his dog's name, then Bige would spring on the bed and lick his mas-

ter's face and hands and fairly bark himself hoarse with joy. Coming up the Brazilian coast Spiller died, and was buried at sea. When the corpse was dropped overboard with a 12-pound shot at its feet Bige tried to leap after it, but was prevented. We locked him up, but he refused food. After two or three days I let him out and sat down on deck with him in my arms. He suddenly sprang away from me and leaped overboard. We shortened sail and lowered a boat, but he refused to be picked up, snapping at the sailors' hands when they attempted to pull him into the boat. It was a deliberate case of suicide, and those old tars cried like children when Bige sank beneath the waves. Had he been a man he would have forgotten his friend in a year. Had he been a woman there would have been a wedding in six months. Yes, I prefer dogs."

[*9 November 1892, p. 7, no. 5*]

No. 23.

"And yet the mother of Stephen Howe, the old ship captain who told that pathetic story of Spiller and his dog 'Bige' at the Lindell the other night was a woman," said a young man in a group last night. "I am glad I haven't lived long enough to forget the lessons of a mother's word and example. The fealty of a dog is the outcome of physical care. It is not so much fidelity as gratitude. The love of woman has passed into a proverb: 'A woman, a dog and a hickory tree; The more you lick 'em the better they be.' The woman first, you see. Last night, on my way down-town I took a short cut through Kerry Patch. The words of Capt. Howe were fresh in remembrance as I passed a saloon not far from the corner of Tenth and Wash. I saw a care-worn woman's face under the electric light waiting patiently for something. A little beyond I met an officer with a lad, 14 years of age perhaps, on his way to the station house. The officer and boy were joined by the woman, the boy protesting and pleading, the mother pale and silent, knowing well how unavailing words were at such a time. But she kept near enough to her son to touch his hand from time to time with its assurance of sympathy. Perhaps he was guilty, perhaps innocent. She was near all the same to comfort. The first was fidelity, the second maternity. I am sorry for Capt. Howe."

[*11 November 1892, p. 7, no. 1*]

No. 24.

"We've got a sure-enough hermit in Hendricks County, Ind.," said John C. Hornsby, of Indianapolis, now at the Laclede. "His name is John Moon. Everybody in Central Indiana has heard of old John Moon. He is about 75 years old, and has been living in a little log hut in a lonely part of the county for more than forty years. The cabin stands in the center of a two-acre patch of ground which is surrounded by an impassable bamboo hedge. Old John boasts that he never rode on a railway train or wore a pair of shoes in his life. He wears the same old suit of patched jeans the year after year. In summer he dons a battered plug hat of the vintage of 1812, and in winter a cap made of squirrel skins. He raises chickens, a little garden truck and shoots small game. He is reckoned the best rifle shot in Indiana. When he is in need of tobacco or a few dimes he digs 'sassafrack root,' as he calls it, and takes it to town. Once each year he tramps to Indianapolis, a distance of twenty miles, to see a circus. He always joins in the parade, and his old plug hat and big, bare feet attract more attention than the drove of elephants or the man-eating tiger. He came from California to Hendricks County. He was a great trapper, hunter and Indian fighter in early days out there, and his hut is filled with the skins of 'grislies' and other savage 'varmints' that fell before his old 'ginger-bread rifle,' as the boys call it. Further than this no one knows anything of his history. He shuns the society of men and was never known to speak to a woman. The country people believe that he has thousands of dollars in gold buried beneath his cabin, the fruits of his early mining ventures and four decades of parsimony. When a boy I was seized with a desire to explore old John's hut and see what it con-

29

tained. Another boy entered into the conspiracy with me and we watched our opportunity. One day old John sallied forth with his rifle to shoot squirrels, and we cut a hole with a hatchet in his Crusoe hedge and crawled through. The one window of the hut was fastened down and the door locked. We had expected this, and brought with us a piece of wire, with which we succeeded in picking the lock. The floor of the cabin was of earth. In one corner was a pile of buffalo and bear skins, which he evidently used for a bed. A black pot and frying-pan stood by the fireplace, and a picture frame hung over it with the face to the wall. We turned it, and found it to be that of a beautiful young woman, dressed in the fashion of half a century ago. It was a haughty face, and reminded me of portraits of the Great Catherine of Russia. The frame was solid silver, and must have weighed 6 or 7 pounds. Beneath the glass, and right across the forehead of the picture, was written in red ink: 'Fair as the lily and false as hell.' "

[*11 November 1892, p. 7, no. 5*]

No. 25.

"The queerest people on this continent are the Hicksites, of Indiana," said W. E. Sanders, a Texas real estate man, who is making a few days' stay at the Southern, waiting for the political earthquake to quiver itself out. "I was raised in Hendricks County, Ind., where Hicksites are thicker'n yellow jackets around a new cider barrel. They are the old Fox Quakers; the original followers of the gentleman who incased himself in a suit of leather and went forth to put a new crinkle in the caudal appendage of the devil. There are but two Hicksite organizations in the State, the rest of the Hoosier Quakers being known as orthodox. The split among the Friends occurred, like many other sectarian bifurcations, over the introduction of the church organ. The young Quakers were inclined to be progressive. They wanted music, pastors and all the modern improvements. The old ones did not take kindly to the innovation, and the Quaker household became divided against itself and has so remained. The queerest thing about the Indiana Quakers is the manner in which they transact their business without recourse to the courts of the country. An Indiana Quaker does not ask the representative of the law for permission to marry or appeal to a legal tribunal for a divorce. He goes to the Church. When he desires to take unto himself a wife he goes before the quarterly meeting and states his case. The matter is taken under consideration and a verdict rendered at the next quarterly meeting. If favorable he becomes a benedict; if unfavorable he accepts his rebuff philosophically and remains a bachelor. Divorces seldom occur among the Quakers, but are not unknown. The party who discovers that marriage is a failure applies to the Church to dissolve the bond. If it sees proper it does so, and there's an end on't. These Quaker marriages and divorces are recognized by the State as legal. Many of the Indiana Quakers are very wealthy. Not believing in bloodshed, they were exempted from military duty, and, while others were handling muskets, they were piling up money. They dominate Hendricks County politically, are all Republicans or Prohibitionists, and will not tolerate saloons. The women wear black poke-bonnets and eschew jewelry. The men dress plainly, are very deliberate of speech and still retain the pronouns 'thee' and 'thou.' But they are by no means as innocent as they look. They are the keenest traders in the world. I would rather attempt to get the best of an Armenian or a Yankee tin-peddler than of a Hicksite."

[*15 November 1892, p. 7, no. 4*]

No. 26.

I began practicing medicine in Southern Indiana thirty-five years ago," said Dr. E. P. Daviss, now a guest at the Laclede. "Money was scarce in those days, and I took my pay in 'chips and whetstones.' There was no other regularly ordained physician in the county, and, as chills and fever were plentiful and the scant population unusually prolific, I was kept pretty constantly in the saddle. A dozen coon skins or a tub of wild honey was frequently my reward for riding twenty or thirty miles. One patron paid me in fence rails, and another made for me a rag carpet. Living on one side of the county were the Smiths and on the other side the Joneses. One morning Père Smith and Père Jones rode up to my front door at the same time and called 'Hullo!' at the same instant. I went out and learned that they had both come in hot haste on the same errand. Each was expecting an early addition to his family, and each wanted the doctor, and wanted him bad. It was twelve miles northeast to the residence of Smith, and thirteen miles southwest to the manor house of Jones. I told them that not being possessed of a Fortunatus hat, I would be compelled to ignore one of the calls. Each insisted that I should go with him. They began to bid against each other. One offered a wagon-load of turnips, two sacks of cornmeal and a side of bacon if I would accompany him, while the other named a barrel of cider, a wagon load of fall pippins and two fat turkeys as the reward of my professional services. 'Now look here,' I said, taking a silver half dollar out of my pocket, 'head is Smith and tail Jones. Here she goes.' I flipped the coin, it came head, and Jones set his spurs into his mule and rode off homeward the picture of despair. Well, sir, sad to say, Mrs. Smith died and her girl baby died. Mrs. Jones presented her husband with a brace of bouncing boys and in two weeks attended church with one on either arm. Smith paid my fee, but he acted as if he wished that half dollar had come tails."

[*18 November 1892, p. 7, no. 8*]

No. 27.

D o you know," said Dr. E. P. Daviss to the corridor man at the Richelieu, "that the most potential factor in the transference of disease germs from place to place and from person to person is the much-coveted 'greenback'? Such is the fact. We use our paper money entirely too long. It passes from hand to hand, from the bank to the counting room, from the gambling hell to the den of vice, from the purse of the small-pox patient to the portmanteau of m'lady—circulating back and forth, gathering up disease germs here, shedding them there, an angel of mercy and an angel of death. In the City of Washington, where the Bureau of Printing and Engraving is located, bright, crisp bills only are to be found in circulation, but the farther we get from that great currency ganglion the more worn, ragged and dangerous does the greenback become, until, when we reach the Pacific, we find it so dilapidated that it can scarce be held together by a liberal use of court plaster. The Treasury stands ready to redeem and destroy these old bills, but no provision exists for their transportation from the holder to Washington. In 1882 Congress passed an act providing for the expressage of worn-out greenbacks, and the result was that the country was quickly supplied with a clean, new circulating medium. The currency act of 1882 should either be revised at the forthcoming session of Congress or some other provision made for withdrawing old disease-bearing bills from circulation. Right here I want to say a word to the ladies, and I hope the *Globe-Democrat* will print it: Never put money of any kind in the mouth. Some ladies have a bad habit of making the mouth a receptacle for everything—hair-pins, buttons, street-car tickets, nickels, etc. I have frequently seen ladies fish an old, dilapidated greenback out of a glove, where it has lain for hours in the moist palm, and hold it between the lips while rebuttoning the glove. Let them pause and consider the travels of that bill. How do they know it is not fresh from the purse of a cholera suspect or the hand of a leper? It may have been worn inside the sock of Sambo or the stocking of a street-walker. It is certainly filthy, and may be reeking with the germs of the most revolting disease known to medical science. Never put money inside the glove. Perspiration opens the pores and increases the danger of inoculation. Never put money in the mouth. It is a filthy habit, to say the least. I would as soon make my mouth the repository of other people's soiled linen as of their money."

[*1 December 1892, p. 7, no. 4*]

No. 28.

It is all luck," said Ralph Moore Wentworth, leaning back in his chair at the Lindell and putting on the air of a misanthrope as his real and genuine imported cigar began to soothe him into talkativeness. "It is every bit luck. I know men who are not half as well posted in my business as I am, and yet are making as much in a month as I am making in a year at the same business. And I am compelled to admit that I know one or two men in my business who in every detail of the work could give pointers and tips twenty-five hours out of the twenty-four, and are merely holding down a subordinate position in the house. 'Energy'? Nonsense. The energy is the same in every instance — each man desiring to improve himself. 'Opportunity'? Well, yes, but what is that but luck? Twelve years ago I laid off one trip because of sickness, and a man who was supposed to be inferior was sent in my place. A wealthy Chicagoan was struck with his 'knowledge of the business,' took him in, started a new house, and to-day — I'm traveling for them. Good firm, too; best in the business. But it is pure unadulterated luck just the same."

[*2 December 1892, p. 7, no. 2*]

No. 29.

No, sir, I repeat it, a real lover never amounted to anything," said Pat Sheridan, as he leaned back and blew rings of smoke to the ceiling, during a discussion of the modern philosophers in the corridors of the Lindell. "They are the only ones who can write love-sick poetry, but I hope you don't call that amounting to anything. What I mean is being great in the ordinary acceptation of the word. You may go through history, from the earliest days to the present, and you will find the great successes are incarnations of selfishness. It has always been that way, and always will be. Eternal vigilance is the price of any success, just as it is the price of liberty; and concentration of thought upon the object in view precludes the possibility of serious love being given elsewhere. Socrates, in his utter indifference to Xantippe; Napoleon, whose ambition relentlessly crushed every human feeling; Goethe, treading the primrose path of dalliance — all are simply samples of the 'great' of earth. Some are indifferent, some tyrannical and some fickle as the bees among the flowers, but all show simply different phases of selfishness. You can not recall a single instance of a name which will stand out against the centuries whose owner was happy in domestic life, and loved his wife and children. The greatest intellect that ever existed recognized this. Lord Bacon said: 'He that hath a wife and children hath given hostages to fortune; for they are impediments to great enterprises, either of virtue or mischief.' It is simply an impossibility for a man to devote himself to ambition and to a loved domestic circle at the same time."

[*3 December 1892, p. 5, no. 4*]

No. 30.

Our 'light literature' is growing both better and worse," said Rev. N. J. Brown, as he turned the pages of the latest "realistic novel" in the corridors of the Lindell. "The execution has improved, but the morale has degenerated. The old innocuous love stories, with a moral tacked on at the end, no longer please. The sweet country girl, the designing villain and the honest-hearted lover have had their day. The idle-hour reader is satiated with such namby-pamby diet. He insists on being shocked. He has turned his back on dreamland and demands realism. He is a-weary of platonic affections and pink-cheeked maidens who, after a narrow escape from the clutches of designing villains, marry the man of their choice and 'live happy ever afterwards.' He wants intrigues with beautiful young wives, duels, railway wrecks, boiler explosions and blazing steamships. He is tired of autumn leaves and spring posies, and demands 'poems of passion.' The more erratic the book the better it sells. A story is told of a young authoress, with a keen eye to business, who re-quested the editor of a great daily to denounce her book as a flagrant violation of the moral code, in order to improve its sale. Whether the story be true or not, certain it is that denouncing a book as indecent is sure to increase the demand for it. It is estimated that barring Tolstoi's 'Kreutzer Sonata' from the mails sold half a million copies of it in America. Enterprising publishers now advertise new books as 'treading close, very close, to the danger line.' Too many of them plunge recklessly across it. To the shame of womankind, be it said, that most of the objectionable works, both in prose and verse, are by female authors. These works are now sold everywhere and are eagerly read by the young of both sexes. They not only corrupt the mind, but they so debauch it that it has no taste for healthy literature. They give the young false views of life. And the great tide of flash fiction is becoming fouler every year. The slums of French and Italian literature are raked and reraked by publishers for unsavory morceaus with which to feed a prurient public appetite. With leave to feed on the fairest of mountains, the public elects to batten on the foulest of moors."

[*6 December 1892, p. 7, no. 6*]

No. 31.

S peaking of money," said John I. Spencer at the Laclede, "brings to my mind the great find the Owens family made near Bedford, Ind., some two years ago. That country is rather hilly and the ground is not very desirable for agricultural purposes. This family had some 200 acres of land and largely used it for pasturage. However, about the time I refer to one of the Owens boys decided to cultivate a small portion which he judged to be better soil than the rest. With this point in view he began plowing in the early spring. In the course of his work he struck a snag. Before turning the plow aside he endeavored to drag out the snag. By striking the horse he forced the plow only deeper into the earth. The sudden start of the horse jerked the sunken log loose from the earth and revealed a heap of silver and gold coins. He gathered the find of coins and removed them to the house, where he polished up the many pieces and took an account of their face value. The find included rare old French coins, both copper, silver and gold; American silver dollars of the 1804 stamp, some Mexican and some coins of the Revolutionary period. The face value of the many pieces footed up $500, but the market value was something like $10,000. The old settlers assert that the money was left there by some former resident, who feared the approach of the Indians. Having buried the money, he probably engaged in a battle with the Indians and never lived to return and take up the gold. The money, no doubt, lay under that log for fully sixty years, and possibly longer. It illustrates the trials of pioneer Western life."

[*14 December 1892, p. 7, no. 2*]

No. 32.

T he finest bits of scenery that I have ever witnessed occur right about the town of Bloomington, Ind., which lies about due east of St. Louis," said Harry Hall, of Mount Clemens, Mich. "The country about there was the earliest settled portion of Indiana, and it now contains the least portion of that State's population. The land is very hilly and full of gravel and rocks. It is, in a great measure, useless for cultivation. The farmers have learned this, and they have left it severely alone, many portions of it having never been plowed at all. This land contains many high hills and rocky ravines that wind about among the hills and lose their waters in underground passageways, only to reappear again at some point farther on, and tumble along over rocks and falls in a most picturesque manner. But one feature that was always interesting to me was the many little graveyards that dot the country. Seemingly every old farm house had a graveyard of its own, and now, the original owners and users being all dead, these little plats of ground are walled in and left to molder and decay. No one thinks of using the rocky land, and so these little spots are perfectly safe from destruction. In some of them a dozen members of the family are buried, the last probably having been laid to rest away back in 1845. Since then many summers of weeds and wild roses have flourished, and little pine trees, that were originally planted for decoration, have grown into tall trees, that forever keep the graves beneath their shadow. While at college there, I have often with a companion entered these sacred precincts, trampled down the weeds and righted the little tombstones, yellow with age, that had long since fallen to earth and buried even the inscribed virtues of the departed deep in the earth. In the winter time, when other trees are leafless, great flocks of crows resort to these pine clumps and create a most noisy rendezvous. I have watched them on cold winter days cawing and screeching in the pine branches, and with every gust of wind flying out and circling about as if unable to hold their position against the wind. So it goes. The hardy pioneers of Indiana's fame are tucked away in little forgotten patches left to the care of the wind and the rain, and furnishing a winter shelter for carrion crows against the cold north winds of January."

[*14 December 1892, p. 7, no. 3*]

No. 33.

"Looking at life in a speculative way," said Charles Heitz, the present Coroner of Cook County, Ill., speaking to friends in the Lindell, "there are any number of men who are perfectly friendless in this world, and I speak from long experience. I have heard the expression that a man's a mighty poor man that has no friends whatever. I want to relate an incident. In September of 1890 the steamer Tioga was blown up at the Washington street bridge, in the Chicago River. The explosion was caused by a dozen barrels of naphtha stored in the hold of the vessel. They were being shipped under a false name to escape heavy freight charges. Not knowing the contents of the barrels, an officer of the steamer visited the hold with a lantern. A leakage had occurred shortly after the stowing of the barrels, and the lighted lantern set flame to the gas. The explosion was terrific, and as a result twenty-nine men lost their lives. The remains of all these men were taken out of the river, burned, blackened and muddy, and inquests were held next day. Eighteen remained unidentified and were removed to the Morgue for a short period. Later the remains were turned over to the medical colleges for use in the dissecting room. Several years have passed since that time, and no one has ever inquired after the remains of those men. In looking up the record not long ago I found the list of twenty-nine, and began to look up the facts in the case again. I found that eleven parties had visited the Morgue after the inquest and picked out their friends. Even these eleven had great difficulty in distinguishing the bodies, and many were uncertain after they had removed and buried the dead that they had secured the right body. But the remaining eighteen remained even uncalled for. We had a full list of the names of the dead. We struck out the name of every body identified and then published the unidentified list. No one ever called for them. It's impossible to believe that eighteen men in one boat had changed their names. No, they were simply homeless and friendless."

[*19 December 1892, p. 5, no. 3*]

No. 34.

I never realized," said Samuel Walters, as he paid for a cigar in the Laclede, "just how many swallows could live in one chimney until a few years ago, when I ran across the knowledge in a country town. They are rather neighborly birds, take them all in all, and I like to see them return. One evening in July some years back I sat on the lawn in front of a friend's house out in Iowa and watched a number of swallows skimming and circling about over the great chimney of a public school close by. My host said that in spring there had been but a few swallows inhabiting the chimney; that they had multiplied rapidly,

and that before fall the sky over the chimney would be black of evenings with the circling birds. I watched them with much pleasure, for if there is anything I enjoy to look at it is to see birds of graceful flight, like buzzards or cranes or swallows. When the shadows fell the birds gathered closer above the school house, and one by one they described a swift circle above the chimney and then dropped, like an arrow, down into the opening. I counted fully 100 before the last one descended. I wondered then how so many birds could inhabit one chimney. Later on in the season, a few days before the opening of the first school term, I met the janitor of the school and we talked birds. Then I inquired about the chimney and the swallows. He said that the chimney would shortly be cleaned for winter service, and that fully 100 vacant nests would be swept down. The birds glue their hard nest of twigs to the chimney sides one above the other in tiers. They live in regular colonies."

[*21 December 1892, p. 7, no. 1*]

No. 35.

Diamonds are rather plentiful now-a-days," began Richard Burlsett, the veteran jeweler, who is registered at the Laclede, "but like really great men, there are very few large ones. We all know of the Koh-i-noor, the whilom treasure of the Khan of Persia. And again the great orange diamond, now in possession of the German Emperor, but the largest diamonds are not always finest. Sometimes a large diamond fails to sparkle properly, lacks radiance and color. Such a stone upon being divided will often make several very brilliant and valuable small diamonds, whose aggregate value would be more than the great colorless original. In the early dawn of civilization diamonds were the cause of more crime than even gold or silver. They have been swallowed for safe-keeping, frequently causing death. Murder after murder can be traced to one or the other of these great diamonds as the primal cause. Some dire State intrigues and plots have had a diamond for the center or nucleus. One of the finest diamonds in the world was found not long since in the Brazilian sands. It came in a novel form. A small quartz rock was found, about the size and shape of an egg, lying in the sands along the bank of the Amazon, in Brazil. This was carried home by a Brazilian peasant, who was attracted by its odd shape and light weight. For some time it lay in his home, with a number of other geological specimens, a mere curiosity. Happening one day in handling it to drop it on a stone block it burst open and lay in halves on the block. The hollow interior that gave the light weight to the stone was filled with blood-red sand. In this sand lay the diamond, a sparkling stone of the rarest quality. The stone was later sold to a diamond merchant and left the finder exceedingly wealthy. It is safe to say that the next egg-shaped stone found in that section will not long remain unbroken, and now that the quality and value of a diamond so formed is well known the next finder will realize a fortune out of it most certainly."

[*21 December 1892, p. 7, no. 2*]

No. 36.

I once stopped in a haunted house," said Albert Jones, while sipping lemonade in the Lindell annex. "That was in the beginning of my theatrical career, some four years ago. I was a rather ambitious young roustabout. I wanted to go on the stage, but somehow my talents were not appreciated by the profession. Then I proposed starting a minstrel troupe of my own, and I did so. With a local companion named Neff, I began making arrangements and soon had a crowd of local talent gathered about me who were ready to accompany me on a tour, and receive their salary in proportion to the net proceeds of our engagements. I ordered lithographs and billed several neighboring towns. Then we started. The Jones and Neff combination, after a successful run of four nights in four different villages, struck Huntington, Ind. We were not rich enough yet to put up at a hotel, but we did the next best thing, we secured a vacant house and slept in that. Every man had his blanket. Oh, we were ambitious; there is no question about that. This house adjoined the Huntington Medical School, and the upper floor was once used for a dissecting room. That's why the house stood vacant. On moving out the students forgot to remove a plain square pine box that lay in one corner, and which contained a well-strung and articulated skeleton. When we discovered the remains we took counsel with one another and discussed the advisability of sleeping elsewhere; but finally we concluded to throw the skeleton out and sleep all together in one room downstairs. There were eight of us, and, after piling the respected departed out into the wood shed, we wrapped our mantles about us, as Bryant says, and lay down to pleasant dreams. My dreams were weird. Finally I awoke and imagined that I heard footsteps up-stairs in the ghost's chamber. Neff lay near me and I shook him. He listened and said that he heard them. Then we awakened the whole company and bade them listen. They did so. We all heard the tramp, tramp, tramp of the ghost above. I rolled up my blanket and prepared to immigrate. So did the company. At last Neff said he heard the stair door open that led down into our room. We immediately adjourned to the yard and surveyed the second floor in the moonlight. We couldn't hear anything nor see anything. We were in quandary as to what to do. The town watch came by and, attracted by the confabulation in the front yard, came in and joined. We told him the circumstances. One member offered him a 'nip of the serpent.' Then he said he would go up and see. We went along. There was nothing up there. We decided to try and sleep once more. With the exception of a few strange noises, that might have occurred elsewhere in the neighborhood, we heard nothing. Next day we secured new quarters and immigrated, but we couldn't explain the footsteps. I do believe it was that skeleton." "What became of the company?" asked a bystander. "It busted at Lafayette, Ind., and I went to Chicago and I've been successful ever since."

[21 December 1892, p. 7, no. 3]

No. 37.

An instance of animal affection came to my notice two years ago," said Aquilla Fleischman, instructor of physics in the University of Kansas, who stopped for a day at the St. James. "It was on the occasion of President Jordan's leaving the State University of Indiana, where I was then a student. President Jordan resigned the presidency of Indiana University to assume that of the Leland Stanford, Jr., University at Pasadena, Cal. While President of the Indiana University Dr. Jordan secured a fine Bernard pup and took good care to raise it properly. The dog soon became proficient in many ways under the tutelage of Dr. Jordan, and seemed to hero worship its master. Nightly the dog could be seen in the

Bloomington Post Office waiting its turn when the mail for the President would be handed out, inclosed in a leathern pouch. With this pouch the dog would trot away toward the residence of the President, and woe to any one who attempted to bar its progress. Dr. Jordan on leaving presented the dog to Prof. Hoffman, of the college. At first the dog was disinclined to part with his master, and upon meeting Dr. Jordan in the street would turn away from Prof. Hoffman and follow after. Being driven away once or twice, however, it made no further attempts at following him. On the occasion of the Doctor's departure Prof. Hoffman, along with the other members of the faculty, went to the depot. The dog journeyed with him. It was here that Dr. Jordan stooped and patted the dog on the head and then entered the cars. The dog watched wistfully for the reappearance of the good Doctor, but in vain. Shortly after this Prof. Hoffman noticed that his dog was absent at a certain period in the day. The operator at the depot also noticed the daily visits of the dog to the station on the arrival and departure of the 2 p.m. train. Being informed as to whom the dog belonged he sent word, and Prof. Hoffman next day watched the strange sight. The dog came, expecting the return of its former master, and waited patiently for the approach of the train. As the train neared the depot it would prick up its ears and observe the arrivals. It was only when the train had passed out of sight that the dog would depart. It was really a touching scene, and shows the depth of animal affection."

[*22 December 1892, p. 7, no. 4*]

No. 38.

I have often wondered," said Francis Estey, at the St. James, "in how much human beings are guided by instinct. Everyone knows that animals are largely regulated by that queer influence we are pleased to name, but very few people believe that it plays any part in human lives. I once had an office cat that came to me a starving kitten. I fed it for the once, and daily it came to the office at the time I arrived, about 9 in the morning, and always very promptly. Once it was stolen from me by a party of clerks, good friends of mine, and they kept it for three months. They told me they had been in the habit of feeding it at noon, and that daily at that hour exactly the cat showed up with remarkable promptness. Then I became interested. I changed the cat's meal hour from 12 noon to 3 in the afternoon and watched the result. Up to that hour the cat was never to be found. At that hour, however, a scratching and clawing occurred at my office door, and my cat was always on time. Now, how did that cat know when it was 9 or 12 or 3 o'clock? We say: 'Instinct; instinct, of course'; but the question still remains unanswered. While I was in college my room contained no clock, and I did not have a watch. My supper hour was 5:30 p.m. and I always left my room at 5. For a while I had to inquire of the landlady the time. Later on, as I studied from 1:30 until 5 in my chair by the window, a queer, nervous sensation overcame me as the hour of 5 p.m. drew near. I always imagined that I was studying over my supper time, and invariably drew on my coat and hurried off to my supper. I can say that in six months I never came a minute too early or late, and I never looked at a clock. Now, that is instinct, of course. I have heard of many such instances, and it has occurred frequently under many conditions, but I must say that instinct is a sure and true guide, and that it plays a great part in the ordinary routine of our daily lives."

[*23 December 1892, p. 7, no. 5*]

No. 39.

The preliminary gathering of crows before they take their flight to the Southland at the approach of winter is always interesting to me," said Frank Gunther, while enjoying a cigar in the parlor of the Lindell. "I do not think that they take their flight from this section of the country, as the winters here are not severe enough. But from the Dakotas and the Southern Cana-

dian Provinces they leave in great numbers after the first severe frosts. One cold frosty morning I arose and looked out of my bed-room window in Red Eric, Dak., down into a neighboring cornfield that was bounded by a rail fence and from which even the dry shocks had been removed. Only the stubble, bleak and frost-covered, remained. The village of Red Eric, Dak., is locally famous for crows. They gather about there in large numbers and obtain considerable food from a neighboring wild rice marsh. I noticed that the tiers of rails, rising seven in number, were thickly sprinkled with crows, perched about and cawing most vociferously. I was rather amused at the spectacle, and stood enjoying it, when I observed a long line of crows approaching from over a neighboring patch of forest. These also settled down within the inclosure. I watched for several hours and continually observed great flocks of crows to come from all directions and gather in the field. By noon the fences and ground fairly swarmed with the birds. It seemed to me there were hundreds of thousands. Then no more came for awhile. The denouement of the whole affair was a great flapping of wings, and, division by division, the great gathering left in harmonious order. It took them fully half an hour before all were under way. When the last flock, or division, took wing, I looked to the south and saw the line dimly fading away into space. Then I knew they were migrating, and I fully un-

41

derstood the beauty of that harmonious simile, 'Like the flight of birds.' "

[*23 December 1892, p. 7, no. 6*]

No. 40.

"No, thanks," said Paul Dresser to a coterie of genials in the parlor of the St. James. "I never smoke, although I like tobacco very well. Why don't I? Well, I'll tell you," continued Mr. Dresser, with a promising smile of a good story. "I once caused the death of a friend of mine by smoking, and since then I have kept a solemn vow never to smoke again. Years ago I was foreman in a powder mill down in Connecticut, about twelve miles from Hartford. I had a good friend who worked under me, a steady, promising young man, and I took considerable interest in him. It was our custom to spend the noon hour together before the mill door eating and chatting. The work in the mill filled the clothes with the powder constituents in great quantities, and in a little while our apparel was highly inflammable. Regardless of this, we were wont to smoke, although we used lid-covered pipes. One day while smoking before the door I opened my pipe to force down the tobacco, seeing that it didn't draw well. My finger knocked some sparks and ashes on my friend's coat, and in a moment his body was enveloped in flames. He jumped and started to run down to the little stream that ran in front of the mill. The wind only fanned the flames more, and by the time he reached the stream he was burned beyond cure. We took him to Hartford, where his wounds were dressed, and where he received the best care, but he only lingered a few days. This fact worked upon me and I have always thought myself guilty of crime in that respect. The young man was so bright and promising that it seemed all the worse to have him die in that manner. I quit smoking then, and I have never touched tobacco since. When a man is young he does not take into account the serious risks that he runs to satisfy a mere moment of desire."

[*24 December 1892, p. 5, no. 4*]

No. 41.

"There are very few people who have not at one time or another laughed at the jests of the goat-joker," said Edward Meinard, to a gathering of artists in the Laclede. "The festive goat is always subject to being punned upon. 'Nanny and William' are consequently always before the public. But really they create a good deal of laughter of themselves. One can not help admiring the sedate nerve which they possess and the manner in which they stroll about inspecting billboards and posters of all kinds, with a seeming intelligence. A laughable peculiarity of the goat is this one fact that it is seemingly given to speculating. With an independent toss of the head it will suddenly stop and gaze about in a leisurely manner, that would almost mean, 'What am I to do next?' As for the tin cans they are supposed to eat, that is not true, but they actually do the next thing to it. They chew off the labels and devour them. I remember an instance that happened in the village of Ellesly, Io. A section boss by the name of Garraghty was given to fostering goats in large quantities. He had a flock of some eleven in all. Garraghty let them loose upon the town of Ellesly, expecting them, of course, to pick up their own living and get fat. For a while they prospered, and then complaints began pouring in from various citizens stating that the goats were breaking into most everything and devouring clothing, etc. Garraghty paid little heed to the complaints. Then one goat disappeared and could never be traced. Shortly after a second disappeared, but a day later, in the night-time, a basket of goat's meat was set at Garraghty's door, and with a note inviting him to try and eat it. It was tough beyond all reclaim. A third was killed and left lying on the common. The citizens had found that Garraghty's goats were poor eating. Then Garraghty killed one, and on examination discovered pieces of half-chewed leather, pulverized wood, can labels, etc., in the stomach. Those goats had been compelled to skirmish for a living, and they did."

[*24 December 1892, p. 5, no. 6*]

No. 42.

"Murder will out, if the moon has to emblazon it,' is the sense of a good old German proverb, and I feel convinced that it speaks the truth," said Etheridge Claflin, who is ensconced at the St. James. "A disappearance occurred many years since near the little town of Silver Lake, Ind., which caused considerable comment at the time and much more some ten years later. A farmer and his wife lived near the banks of the Silver Lake at that place, and in 1872 they suddenly disappeared. The furniture was left intact, but nothing was found that would give a clew to their whereabouts. Years rolled by, and the house with the lapse of time was vested with a superstitious garb that included the vagaries of a hundred garrulous washerwomen, who claimed to have seen this and that and the other most marvelous thing within the immediate precinct of the forsaken dwelling. In 1881 a farmer named Arnold, driving from Claypool to Silver Lake, a distance of six miles, came up with a little old man dressed in black, who trotted along the road path with his eyes bent toward the ground. In a neighborly mood, Arnold called to him, proffering him a 'lift,' as it is termed, for a portion of the distance. The man never answered. 'Will you ride, stranger?' called Arnold, driving close beside him. Suddenly the horses, on drawing so close to the stranger, whose face Arnold could not see, shied and broke into a gallop. Being an expert with the reins, Arnold checked the flying team, and, looking back, saw that the stranger had disappeared. This rather surprising incident occurred to other residents of the country who were wont at eventide to travel from Claypool to Silver Lake. The queer little man in black became the gossip of many tongues and the particular places of his appearance and of his vanishing were accurately fixed. He disappeared not far from the vacant cottage so long the sacred temple of all the uncanny witch lore that the village could rake together. Here, also, a little stream wended over the roadway down to the lake. There was no bridge. The wagons simply drove through. A farmer desiring a load of sand drove to the little stream to gather it from the banks. His excavations revealed the bones of a skeleton. The authorities were notified, the bones were removed, and an examination made. It came out that a woman had been murdered, her head crushed, and her body buried in the sand. This recalled the disappearance and the mysterious man in black. Six months later a dispatch came from the authorities of Tucson, Ariz., stating that a man hung for murder there had confessed on the gallows to butchering his wife near Silver Lake, Ind., and burying her body in the sand. The skeleton now lies buried in the graveyard at Silver Lake, and it is a source of dire alarm to any inhabitant who is compelled to travel that way after dark."

[*27 December 1892, p. 5, no. 4*]

No. 43.

I tell you," said L. U. Zahn, who is spending the holidays at the Lindell, "a person gets to longing for home these Christmas days and the longing becomes almost excruciating pain. To see people crowding the streets with smiling faces and carrying bundles just as merrily as though they weren't heavy at all makes a person think of friends they must have and then of the friends one has, and that is what brings on the blues so bad. I was over in Illinois a few days ago in the little village of Martha. I ran over to a friend and only remained two days. But in that time I took a stroll out among the leafless woods and scrambled over rail fences and dead logs, returning to the town across the fields and through a graveyard. I stopped on a hill that looks down on the village, and pondered over the loneliness of the scene. The light had faded out of the sky and the lamps began to appear and shine out through the windows of the warm little houses. After a little the village was entirely enshrouded, all but for the myriad of shining lamps. Those lights gleaming through the mist and the darkness made me feel more lonely than ever. They brought back a vision of another house in a village which was mine, and of smiling parents and all that until I got the blues. Then I hurried in, and, gathering my grip, returned to St. Louis. I don't mind being alone in a hotel in a large city. The crowd and the rush somehow keep a man company, but to visit alone a country town — well, that's more than I can stand."

[*29 December 1892, p. 7, no. 1*]

No. 44.

"Talk about fame and honor and all that," began John M. Maxwell to a *Globe-Democrat* reporter, "I have almost got over all that. A man that gets above starvation nowadays is doing excellently well, but the man that lays up $20,000 is really successful, although I didn't think so a few years ago. In those days I was given to writing poems about the fading shadow, beautiful snow, etc. I had three or four plays, some thirty poems, the half of a comic opera, two philosophical essays, the first three chapters of a long novel all written and a salary of $12 a week. I was given to reading 'Thanatopsis' and Carlyle's 'Hero Worship,' and the more I read the more inflamed I became at my poor position in life. Eventually I decided to cap the climax and write an epic poem and then starve to death. The world would then find out what a master mind had lived unappreciated. Well, sir, that epic was the making of me. I let it occupy all my spare moments and shirked my work to go off in a corner and write a few lines about the great trombones smashing the heavenly spheres together. The result was that I got fired from my position as collector for an easy-payment firm and went forth to seek a job. Then I eased up on literary work. I didn't have half the ambition to starve to death and let the world discover my masterpieces when I should lie a stiff and soulless corpse, not half. All I wanted was due assurance that I was going to eat regular. Well, my quest didn't pan out well, and I began to worry most fearfully. To close it all the house where I roomed caught fire and all my brainy efforts evaporated in smoke. That completed my reformation. When I secured work in a wholesale dry goods house I earned my salary and studied to learn the business. I have had better luck since then and now I'm a commercial tourist. I don't want to discourage any literary genius, but, by the way, I don't think a real literary genius could be discouraged or turned aside at all."

[*29 December 1892, p. 7, no. 2*]

No. 45.

"It often happens," said Horace Croxton in the parlor of the Richelieu, "that men have only a moderate development of the sense of propriety and the eternal fitness of things, while yet possessing great culture and charming personal characteristics. It happened once that a reception was given to a prominent college professor in the town of Easton, Kan. He was a man of wide educational fame, the Vice President of

45

a university, and, besides all, an ex-minister. Great preparations were made for a swell affair, and all the prominent citizens were invited. A delicious luncheon was served, after which all the guests gathered in the parlor to enjoy some select readings and recitations. These were concluded at about 10:30 p.m. At this time a much-respected guest arose and said that he would now ask the professor to address a few remarks to the audience. Prof. D. was deeply interested in explaining some formulae to a lady friend and failed to catch the drift of the invitation. From the manner in which the guests looked at him he concluded — of all things most ridiculous — that the reception was at an end and that he had been asked to invoke a blessing. With a solemn countenance he stood by his chair, closed his eyes and asked the Lord to extend his mercy to all members present. A few guests equally lost to the general fitness of things took the prayer as an intended joke. No sooner had the learned gentleman opened his eyes than he was greeted with smiles and laughter that caused his optics to distend even wider than usual. The whole affair was spoiled. There was no remaining alternative. The reception was forced to end, to avoid an awkward and tasteless explanation. The joke went round for weeks until it reached the professor's ears, who, strange to say, took the matter as a good joke. But it seems queer that people with splendid culture and environment seem to utterly lack that sense of propriety

that with many uneducated persons seems almost an instinct."

[*29 December 1892, p. 7, no. 3*]

No. 46.

Seen queer things in my life?" began K. D. Loomis to the clerk of the Laclede. "Certainly I have, and very strange things. The strangest of all things that ever interested me was the will-o'-the-wisp, that indistinct, pale light that hurries over swamp lands and down in forsaken marshes. I was once an engineer on the Pennsylvania road, and on my midnight runs across Ohio and Indiana I have seen those strange lights frequently. They are counted omens of the direst calamities, and very few engineers who have ever made their acquaintance doubt the result of their signals. Rushing through the night, when all the inhabitants are at rest and no light of any kind visible, I have sat and looked out over the still fields for lack of anything better to do. Then it was that I often caught sight of these strange phosphorescent glimmerings away off in some fields bobbing along much as greyhounds leap, and then the train would carry me out of the range of their wanderings. If they ever cross the path of your engine it's a sure sign that trouble is ahead. I remember once one followed my train for a distance of nine miles before breaking company with it. It was where the Pennsylvania crosses the great Kankakee swamp in Indiana. The light came out from a patch of brush and swung lightly along side by side with the engine and not over twenty yards to the left of it. We were making thirty-five miles an hour, and that will-o'-the-wisp seemed hardly to move, and yet it was always beside us. After some nine miles it disappeared again. If it had crossed the track I would have slowed up and looked for trouble before the end of my run. You can't see how a light could go thirty-five miles an hour and not move, can't you? Well, it does it just the same, just as the moon keeps up with you when you run or walk, and the moon doesn't seem to move fast, does it?"

[*30 December 1892, p. 7, no. 3*]

No. 47.

I was once lost in a cave," said Charles Brandon, dropping his pen in the writing-room of the Lindell and turning smilingly towards a *Globe-Democrat* reporter. "My experience is laid in Kentucky, where I visited some friends a year ago. I was always anxious to explore a cave, and when I heard of the near proximity of one I proposed to visit it. One morning I asked Harris, my friend, to lead the way, and he did. We bought several hundred yards of sheep twine, trimmed up a couple of

torches and wended our way to the cave. The entrance was a rocky aperture in the side of a beautiful wooded hill, and we slipped down to the first landing in a trice. Some little distance in we fastened the twine and then moved on. The twine gave out just where our progress led us to a large arched aisle like that of a church. We did not turn back, however. Here we set up a tall white stalagmite that had fallen to earth, and tied to it the end of our twine. About a hundred feet farther on the aisle ended and a ragged, perpendicular wall arose. We climbed this, hand over hand. At the top was an opening that looked through into a great chamber and down into the smooth surface of an underground stream. We crawled through and I sat down near the entrance. Harris climbed down to the stream. I wanted to keep near to the entrance so as not to lose track of it. After watching Harris moving about in the distance for a few minutes I glanced about to take a reassuring glance at the aperture. I could not see it. I made a move toward the place, but the entrance was not there. I looked about, and further on I saw several, but I knew that I had not moved away 10 feet. My nerve departed. In an instant I felt clammy and cold. Then I cried out to Harris. The hollow sound of my voice astounded me. Harris came hurrying up to the rocky ledge and stood beside me. 'What's the matter?' he said. 'I can't find the entrance that we came through,' I exclaimed. We both looked, but in vain. It was gone. We looked at one another with blanched faces. I murmured something about 'awful,' and Harris simply weakened and sat down. I had visions of death, of chattering ghosts in that miserable vale, of starving to death and of wandering about in that rocky blackness, a mumbling, chattering maniac. The more I thought the weaker I became. The blood rushed to my head. I lost my balance and sunk down. When my head struck the rock I was wide awake. My torch was sputtering on the ground. I looked about. Right before me I saw the entrance way. I might have rolled through it. Then I jumped up and it was gone again. But I knew the trick. It was hidden by an overhanging ledge and that was why I could not see it. We crawled through and hurried along the aisle. We untied the twine and followed it a great deal faster than we had entered. Regardless of bumps and bruises we hurried on and reached the entrance. Then we climbed out. I rejoice in the memory of that experience. Yet I don't care to repeat it. The memory is plenty for me."

[*30 December 1892, p. 7, no. 4*]

No. 48.

"The beauty of socialism is that it is simply despotism without the despot," said Eugene Thralls, who is at the St. James. "I came to this conclusion after my recent tour through Russia and Turkey. In Russia we see the fundamental principle of socialism in full operation, namely, Government control of everything. The fact that the Government is one man does not detract from the strength of the principle. In Russia the Government owns and controls the railways, the telegraph, telephone, postal service, press, street traffic, street lighting and almost everything. But of course these things are not controlled in the interest of the people, but rather in the interest of the Emperor. Hence the trouble. Russia would make a most delightful socialistic community if the Emperor could be suddenly done away with and the people as suddenly educated. The Government controlling everything, it would only be necessary to transfer the control to the people's choice and you would have a kind of Utopia. The thing might be worked inversely and a fine socialistic community transformed into the most despotic form of government, with the reins all in one man's hands, but that would not be likely to happen where people have once gained any kind of an intellectual status."

[*2 January 1893, p. 5, no. 1*]

No. 49.

If a man wants to be thrown into himself, as it were," said M. E. Anderson, one of a party bound for Old Mexico, now at the Lindell, "he wants to visit that indispensable medical college annex, the dissecting room. It is in such a place that man realizes what a frail, miserable thing he is and how easily he may even lose his identity here on earth. Not long since I was invited to visit one by a medical friend. I started out at 7 in the evening and tramped through a heavy snow to the college. The exercise made me feel rather buoyant, and I ascended the steps to the room in question in rather a merry mood. The door of the dissecting room stood wide open, but the stair was curved, and stopping three steps from the top landing I could see a long line of feet protruding over the edge of fifteen parallel tables. A strong odor of disinfectant floated out to my nostrils. Well, just that much of the scene caused me to halt and hesitate whether to go in or no. At length I picked up courage enough to pass in. I don't care to recall the worn, shrunken faces and limbs of the twenty-eight unknown dead. But the after reflections of that half hour are permanent and valuable. Where so many friendless beings could be gathered from seemed worthy of study. How many souls had here departed without even a friend to claim their clay. I often wonder now if some one of them did not at some period in his life do some act of char-

ity, some deed of kindness, that would endear him to the beneficiary's opinion so at least to assure himself a decent burial. The whole thing seemed barbarous and even sacrilegious to me."

[*2 January 1893, p. 5, no. 3*]

No. 50.

I notice that the reformers are still busy inventing panaceas for poverty," said Maj. Mike Looscan as he joined the circle of nation-savers in the corridors of the Laclede. "They have been at it ever since Lycurgus' time, but, like the secret of perpetual motion, it still remains both a hidden quality and an unknown quantity. Something like a thousand infallible catholicons for the ills this earth appears to be heir to have been discovered in as many years; yet, notwithstanding the wonderful fecundity of social therapeutics, m'lady continues to add to her store of jewels and the workingwoman finds it ever harder to earn an honest crust. To toil and suffer is the primal, eldest curse, and no nation, race or tribe has yet been able to evade it. There will never be an 'equal distribution of wealth' until there is an equal distribution of brain and muscle—until all men have the same faculty of producing and saving. Even then accident and incident would make some millionaires and some paupers. 'The poor ye have ever with you,' despite the protests of reformers for thirty centuries that it is altogether unnecessary. It were the part of wisdom to distrust the reformer who insists that he can cure all social and industrial ills, and do it while you wait."

[*3 January 1893, p. 5, no. 1*]

No. 51.

I had an exciting experience once," said Walter Odell, who is at the St. James, "and it not only thrilled me but all those who witnessed it. I was superintending the construction of a library building at Evansville, Ind. The building is a beautiful affair, massively constructed and one that took a long time to build. We had great blocks of granite to move and elevate. We lifted them all the way from 1 to 80 feet. One particular block was to complete a corner decoration and it was truly a massive affair. The stone was caught up in the great iron tongs attached to the derrick and some one was compelled to stand on the stone and balance it as it ascended. My men seemed rather diffident in the matter, so I, more to give them an example than anything else, stepped up on the stone and told them to heave away. The little engine was started, and aloft I swung up and toward the high corner, fully 60 feet in the air. As I neared the corner I suddenly felt my base give way, and before I could grip my hands I had slipped down to the hooks and re-

mained hanging there. Meanwhile the men below stood gazing, seemingly dumfounded at the accident. I could see them from my awkward position, and I shouted a command to reverse the engine and lower me to the ground. It was only my quick order that awakened them to a perception of my condition. When I reached the ground I was mad enough to discharge the entire crew. The second time the stone was elevated they all refused point-blank to have anything to do with it. I took my position again, and this time safely balanced the block and placed it neatly. But I never will forget my sensation, hanging as I did, 60 feet in the air by my hands."

[*7 January 1893, p. 5, no. 5*]

No. 52.

A very queer occurrence passed under my immediate observation some eight years ago," said Russell Ratliff to a *Globe-Democrat* reporter in the Lindell. "It was during the blasting for the great Mackinac tunnel, that connects Canada with Northern Michigan. At the time this incident happened the tunnel was well under way, some 1000 feet having been blasted out and the walling of that portion had already begun. Blasting rocks in a tunnel is not the most pleasing labor in the world, nor is it the safest, still you can almost hire men to commit suicide these days. Well, this work of blasting was being carried on by a squad of ten men and being carried on very successfully. By some accident in the process of blasting a portion of giant powder was unintentionally set off, and the result was a grand blast in which rocks flew about quite promiscuously. No one was hurt, however, as there was not enough of it to cause the tunnel to cave in. I may say here that sound doesn't travel through rock to any extent. You slap a brick against the rock wall of a tunnel, and instead of the sound passing away through the rock, it rolls along the great corridor, seemingly increasing in volume, roaring and reverberating, until the din is almost deafening. At the time this charge exploded the men stood some distance back, and when the sound had rolled on past they peacefully resumed their work. Now, at the same time a party of visitors were approaching through the tunnel— three men they were. The fact is that this explosion sent a great volume of sound rolling out towards the light, which increased at every step. The roar of that explosion was so great when it reached the approaching parties that it completely ruined their sense of hearing, for the time being. They were perfectly deaf and remained so to my positive knowledge for over three years. One of them, who probably did not have an extra good sense of hearing at the time, has not recovered yet, and it is doubtful if he ever will. The other two partly regained their hearing and in time will probably recover it fully. I may add that you could not induce those three gentlemen to enter a tunnel again, even at barrel-end of a revolver."

[*15 January 1893, p. 7, no. 5*]

No. 53.

"Walking in one's sleep is one of the most dangerous and still one of the most unavoidable habits that a person can have," remarked Victor A. Spaulding to the Corridor reporter in the parlor of the Lindell. "I did it for a long while, but eventually outgrew it, much to my satisfaction. Why, I have often awoke in the dead of night and found myself strolling about the house, sometimes with my face pressed against a wall with a painful feeling in my head, as though I had just bumped it. I have caught myself tramping down dark stairways, much as one might imagine a ghost to come prowling down from a haunted chamber. The cold, damp clay of cellar rooms, has often been the means of awakening me, but the strangest awakening that I ever had was at my old home in Warsaw, Ind. We had a large old-fashioned two-story frame house there, and I had a bed room in the northwest corner of the house on the second floor. From this room I nightly issued and tramped about the house, invariably receiving some bumps or bruise as a memento of my tour. One night I awoke with a remarkably clear perception of things, so I thought, for I was wont to feel dazed and sleepy on other nights. I looked about me. I was lying on my side on the ground, clad only in my night garments, and close to the north wall of our home. It was a warm summer night, and the moon shone beautifully full and clear through the swaying branches of an apple tree through which I gazed at it. I looked about, and saw that I lay directly below my window. Then, and this is the most remarkable thing about the occurrence, severe pains seized me in my arms, shoulders and breast. I felt seriously wounded, and began to groan in agony. My groans brought the family delegation out into the moonlight, and they carried me in. A physician was called, who examined me and said that I was only severely stunned. He left a sleeping potion, and the next morning I felt all right. But what strikes me as remarkable is the fact that I did not feel the fall nor the pain until so many seconds after I was awake."

[*16 January 1893, p. 5, no. 6*]

No. 54.

"Spiritualism is my hobby now," said Frank H. Wakefield, of Detroit, at the Laclede yesterday. "It has been ever since I heard of that fellow up in my own State who is going to prove to the world that his theory is the only correct one. This particular spiritualist lives in Muskegon, and is in the last stages of consumption, likely to go off any day. He is hoping to prove positively to his friends still in the material state that his spirit will exist after it has separated from his body. Some time ago he went to Pittsburg and had a glass cylinder made especially for him. It is so constructed that it can be sealed air-tight in a second's time. In this cylinder he has suspended with fine copper wires two pieces of metal so light that they can be brought into contact with each other by the slightest motion of the air within the cylinder. These wires pass through the cylinder, one being connected with a battery and the other with a telegraphic instrument. He has made arrangements with his friends at his death and just before the spirit leaves his body, to seal him up in this cylinder that his spirit may be prevented from taking its departure, and at the same time he will be enabled by a series of systematic disturbances of the air within the cylinder to communicate with his friends by means of the telegraph instrument. If the experiment proves a success his friends, at the end of three days, are to open the cylinder and let his spirit take its flight. I don't know what his arrangements are in case of failure, as he hasn't taken failure into account. If he wins there'll be some few converts to his doctrine I assure you."

[*17 January 1893, p. 7, no. 5*]

No. 55.

I have often heard young authors complain," said Adam Corwaith to a *Globe-Democrat* reporter while lounging in the Lindell, "that men who have attained fame and wealth in a literary way are cold and even harsh to their still striving brothers. This is probably true, but without consideration of certain necessitous rules that must govern every literary man it would seem to be a blot on the fair fame of the superior minds of the age. An author who has attained fame in a literary way is the constant recipient of manuscripts which he is requested to read and edit for the striving genius and author, and to pass on it a favorable criticism, or he is counted a ninny and a much overestimated crank. The second worry that a successful author is subjected to is the letters which usually accompany these manuscripts, and the third is the begging letter. An author who will read all the manuscripts of plays, poems, novels, etc., that are daily sent to him will soon doubt his own originality. He will daily read new ideas that were probably in his own mind before, and then if he sees what was originally his own thought the person who sent the manuscript in which the parallel thought was included will immediately cry plagiarist. A continuation of such a liberal policy will result in constant doubt and worry to the conscientious author, who is seeking new ideas and yet wishes to keep from treading upon the sensitive feet of the aspiring applicant. So a young author soon learns that he owes it to himself and to his fame to refuse consistently to read any manuscript sent, or to answer any letters, for it would simply be to sow the wind and be annihilated in a storm of budding ideas. This is the source from which the many complaints of hard-hearted men of genius come from, but the source is not a just one, and I constantly maintain that the famous authors are, as a rule, the most liberal of men."

[*17 January 1893, p. 7, no. 6*]

No. 56.

The most practical Spiritualist I ever heard of," said Mr. George Poston, at the Lindell, "is an old man named John Hall, who lives on a farm or claim near Helena, Mont. A number of years ago Hall's wife died. He refused to believe she was dead, and kept the body in the house for several weeks before he would consent to have it buried. He still declares that his wife is not dead and that she is with him continually. His only daughter married and removed to another State soon after her mother's death, and since that time the old man has lived alone, leading the life of a hermit. He has never cut his hair nor beard since that time, and both are now fully 2 feet long and almost white. At every meal he places two chairs, and prepares food for two. He holds conversations with an imaginary person, who he calls Mary, his dead wife's name, and acts and talks in all things as though his wife was living with him in the flesh. He declares that she has grown young again and looks as she did when he wooed and won her. He consults her spirit about all things and says that he hears her voice as plainly as that of any living person, and always grows angry and excited when any one attempts to convince him that he is the victim of a delusion. 'Why, man,' he will say, 'don't you see her? There she is in that chair. She will never die and neither will I. She tells me that I will grow young again as she is.' He insists that she tells him there is a rich gold mine on his claim which he will one day work and will make him the richest man in the world. The old fellow knows nothing about spiritualism, and on all other subjects he is perfectly sane, but I never saw or heard of an individual so thoroughly imbued with spiritualistic faith. By his neighbors he is regarded as a harmless crank whose mind was unbalanced by his wife's death, and has come to be called by them 'The Gold Spook.' "

[*18 January 1893, p. 7, no. 7*]

No. 57.

I made a queer and very interesting experiment with a growing corn stalk," said Harvey Samuels as he settled in one of the great rockers in the Lindell. "I had always heard a great deal about the effect of injecting medicines and food into human beings, the method being pronounced preferable and more beneficial in case of extreme illness than that of feeding through the regular channels. My work with this corn plant was decidedly interesting. I secured a small glass syringe with a very fine point to it. After the corn was two weeks and only a few inches tall I began to inject the unfermented juice of crushed apples. My first injection was not quite a drop. Three days later I repeated the dose, increasing it slightly. In a little while the injection was a daily occurrence and the dose increased proportionately. The corn stalk waxed fat and tall. All along it gave promise of great size and large fruit. Its height in July was fully 16 inches above the tallest stalk in the field. Its ears were much larger, while the silken tassel was much smaller, and lacked the depth of color characteristic of the other plants. I took an ear home to steam and eat. I can tell you that the quality of that corn for eating purposes was excellent. It smacked a little of apple, just the slightest suggestion of it, and not at all disagreeable, as one might suppose. The grains were large and juicy. In fact, the quality of the corn was far superior to anything I had ever eaten in that line. Next summer I am going to repeat the experiment. I will also try the effect of potato juice, and see if I can not tend to a small patch in this manner, so that I will have enough for eating purposes at least."

[*20 January 1893, p. 7, no. 3*]

No. 58.

I was one of the first to discover gold in the Ember district of New South Wales," said Harold Meyer, a wealthy citizen of Australia, who is stopping at the Lindell. "The fact that gold existed there was not known until 1884, when I announced my discovery by staking my claim and beginning operations. My discovery was purely accidental. It was rather interesting, also, you'll agree. I own a large cattle ranch in the Ember district, a very fertile territory, to say the least. For my own accommodation I dug a well, and some 9 feet down I struck quite a small stream, that fed the well most excellently. One day, some two months after the well had been finished, I accidentally dropped a magnet into it. I tried in a dozen different ways to secure it again, but to no purpose. Finally I gave the matter up in disgust. Some three weeks later I visited Sydney, and while there thought to secure a magnet. When I reached home I immediately prepared to recover the old one. I lowered my purchase, fastened to a cord, down into the well and slowly moved it about. After three-quarters of an hour of such desultory fishing I felt that I had a double load of something, and pulled up. It was my magnet, but apparently wofully changed. It was covered completely with shining particles that I could not immediately explain. Upon examination I found that they were gold. I repeated the experiment, and in twenty-four hours the magnet made quite a showing. Of course I began investigating various portions of the land, and soon found that I had a rich tract. I formed a company and named the mine 'The Golden Magnet.' That's how I have made my money, and I expect to make a few cents more before I die."

[*20 January 1893, p. 7, no. 5*]

No. 59.

I heard not long since an excellent lady, of splendid culture and broad knowledge, remark," said J. A. Fielding to a *Globe-Democrat* reporter, "that music to her was no more than the clatter of drum-sticks, and that she could not appreciate at all any of the delicious strains that people talk about and praise. Her remark did not surprise me much, for I know that many ears lack the power to appreciate the divine sweep of the harp as much as some eyes lack the power to detect the glories of color and the expressions of character in a face. But her remark carried me back to a scene in Southern Texas, a railroad camp, one Sunday morning in May, when all the men were idle and speculating on what to do. I remember that on that morning fully fifty men, rough, hard-working railroaders, whose life lacked all of the elements of refinement and culture, and all the elevating influences of marriage and home, gathered to hear a strolling minstrel, a deformed pedestrian through this world of ours, who carried a violin and possessed a sweet rich voice. His musical efforts were received first with boisterous jokes and rough remarks, but later on the crowd was hushed into silence as his rich voice sang in time with the strains of the violin. 'Old Lang Syne' was included in his repertoire as well as 'Annie Laurie.' The last hushed all into stillness. Then the singer struck up 'Home, Sweet Home,' and threw all the passionate longing of an outcast and a stranger into the movements of his bow and glory of his voice. That strong, rough body of men were moved beyond description. There was more than one throat that felt choked and more than one eye that was wet with an unbidden tear. Some one said, 'Let's sing the chorus, boys,' and fifty voices, little in harmony, broke out into a soulful tribute to the grandest of all God's creations, the American home. As I thought of that I wondered what the effect would have been on my lady friend could she have been there, and I pitied her for her great loss in not being able to appreciate that best one-third of this life of ours, music."

[*23 January 1893, p. 5, no. 5*]

No. 60.

"Y ou're having very fine skating here in St. Louis," said W. L. Willey, as he looked out from the Southern into Market street and watched the foot passengers hug themselves in a vain endeavor to keep warm. "I enjoyed skating myself for a number of years, but one accident that followed in train of my skating mania rather quenched all further desire for pleasure in that line. It happened four years ago at my old home, near Pesanga, Me. Maine is full of lakes, full of rough, rich scenery that is pleasant to look on at all times of the year. Gray Rock Lake was always my favorite skating place. I went there in preference to any spot the district afforded. Many a time I have buttoned up at 9 in the morning, when the sun was just bright enough to make everything sparkle, but not warm enough to make anything melt, and have tramped away alone to Gray Rock to skate. Why, I would linger on that beautiful crystal sheet until the sun sank in the west, running races with my shadow, cutting great circles in the clear, greenish ice and gliding along much as one imagines a swallow must glide downward on the air. One day I, with a neighbor companion, was spending the afternoon that way when in the course of one of my sharp turns I felt as though the earth had been jerked away, and I shot down into bitter-cold water. When I came up again my head struck against some opposing force. The whole situation rushed into my conception with terrific force and pain. I was under the ice. I don't remember much of what followed except of vainly struggling and buffeting in a wild, aimless manner. When I came up for the first time I had not missed the opening very far; the second time I came up I did not miss it at all. My head rose above the ice. Then my companion acted. I was drawn out and simply dragged by him to a neighboring cabin. Of that part I don't remember anything. It was fully two months before I recovered from the effects of that bath. I had lung fever and brain fever and almost everything else in the catalogue of worldly ills. Since then, I have gainsaid my desire, sometimes intense, to strap on a pair of steels and just glide about a little. However much my lesson taught me, the sight of ice always revives that beautiful lake of Maine and the happy hours that I spent racing my shadow."

[*23 January 1893, p. 5, no. 6*]

No. 61.

W hy is it?" said Emil Mueller, a Boston musician, at the Laclede yesterday. "Why is it that women do not excel as musicians? I see that Prof. Otis T. Mason has been examining a lot of American aboriginal musical instruments, and in all the lot he has not found a single instrument that would have been peculiar to women. Even those of the men he has found were never played upon by women. Women have never done anything in

the way of composition that is calculated to last twenty-four hours. It is a funny thing, the very branch in which we would expect to see a woman shine is music, and yet she does not figure in it to any appreciable extent whatever."

[*24 January 1893, p. 7, no. 1*]

No. 62.

O f course we are interested in science," said Julian Reed at the Lindell yesterday. "But science has its drawbacks. In the words of the cynic, posterity has done nothing for us. We lament the fact that, like a spendthrift, we today, boasting ourselves the greatest of all the ages in intelligence, are simply pulling down instead of building up. We are consuming nearly a hundred-fold the just supplies to which we are entitled. As heirs of all the geological aeons we simply receive this intelligence in trust for future generations. Every succeeding triumph of science merely leads to a more rapid exhaustion of the garnered store of the earth. In ten or twelve generations the coal fields of Great Britain shall have been exhausted, and the forests and woods are suffering from a wanton waste. The death of the earth and sun shall both come. Then will come the end of human life. That is a common theory, but the human race is taking pains that this shall come to pass thousands of years before it should. The greatest of the earth's hoarded

57

stores in this country, petroleum and natural gas, have been practically exhausted in this generation alone. In 150 years Great Britain will have 300,000,000 people, more than can live together, less than 6 square feet of earth apiece to live on. It's awful, but then that's 150 years hence, and we may as well be happy while we may and have done with worrying."

[*24 January 1893, p. 7, no. 8*]

No. 63.

T alking about mineral waters," said Ryan Tillman, as he eased the nip of the serpent with a finger of seltzer at the bar of the Laclede, "I got enough of mineral water in one trip to Mount Clemens last summer to satisfy me forever. I went to Mount Clemens to see that a friend of mine should be comfortably located, seeing that he was too crippled up to look after himself. On the second day of my stay, while I was preparing to leave town, I struck a friend of mine from Montreal, who advised me to take a bath for fun; said a mineral bath would make me feel better. I decided that I would try the water, and that evening soaked myself. That night I was seized with a severe attack of acute rheumatism. Oh! I was all done up. They called a doctor. I related my experience, assured him that I had never had a touch of rheumatism in my life before, and that I had had no premonition of ill-

ness. He said it was that one bath I had taken; that acute rheumatism was inherent in my system, and that before many years it would have made its appearance. Well, I took the baths for acute rheumatism, and in three weeks I was out and around again. I'll admit that I felt younger and better after than before, but I never could realize how a mineral bath could draw out an inherent disease that had no intention of coming out for several years."

[*25 January 1893, p. 7, no. 4*]

No. 64.

N ever seen a fish asleep, eh?" said Cornelius Hinman, who is located at the Lindell. "Well, I have. I've seen them sleep sound and much to their sorrow, especially catfish. There is nothing more wary than a fish. You know that you can't creep up on them nor drop a pebble anywhere within 50 feet of them but what they will dodge away; that is, when they are not asleep. How I come to know so much of this is that I have caught them without bait when they were sleeping, although I did use a hook and line. The first one that I ever caught this way was a large catfish that I observed daily to be in one particular spot—the base of a wooden pile that supported an icehouse chute that led out into the water. A kind of nest was there, a depression in the mud, and here that catfish was to be found every day at about 2 p.m. It would lay for hours in the rays of the afternoon sun and never move. I decided to catch it. First I fished around there day after day, but to no purpose. Bait of any kind wasn't any inducement to that catfish. I concluded that it must be asleep, when it would allow a fat minnow to swim by and never touch it. I got a sharp plain hook, which I properly weighted, so that it would act direct. I lowered it and moved it slowly up to the side of the fish. Then I turned the line so that the hook was directly under it. Then I gave a quick jerk; the catfish darted away, but not very far. I had him foul, and all because he was sleeping. I have caught pike and sunfish the same way at least a dozen different times."

[*25 January 1893, p. 7, no. 6*]

No. 65.

S peaking of people who are the victims of passion or of a habit," said Olney Wade, of Elizabeth, N.J., who is at the Lindell, "the most remarkable case I know of was that of a young Dane by the name of Christian Aaberg, who came to America in 1883. This young fellow, not over 26, was the son of a Danish nobleman, a member of the Danish Parliament and a man of high intellectual accomplishments, coupled with suave refinement. The characteristics of the father were those of the son, with the exception of the son's passionate nature, which led him to many excesses, of which the most prominent was that of drink. His father tired of his wild escapades at home, and bestowing an annuity on the young man forced him to leave the country. He came to New York, where I met him. His career was a remarkable one. He plunged into everything sensuous and debilitating. His annuity he sold for temporary pleasure, and at last found himself compelled to look for work or starve. He secured a position running the elevator for the firm I now represent. This Dane could talk on the most inspiring themes. His knowledge was seemingly limitless, and his discourses on the purpose of life, the affinity of character and like subjects were marked by sincere thought and appreciation. Through the Danish Consul at Washington he communicated with his father, and after many promises secured $70,000. With this he bought a small but really beautiful farm in Pennsylvania and went to live on it. The closing chapter of the story was that he was found in his room some few months after in a drunken stupor. The table was set with the finest of wines and liquors, and mingled with them were books by the master minds of the world. He had drank himself literally to death, for he never awoke from that condition."

[*27 January 1893, p. 7, no. 5*]

No. 66.

I have never been inconvenienced by a strike of any kind except once," said Mark M. Strafford in the corridor of the Lindell. "I have never employed labor to any extent, and so have kept out of the range of disgruntled employes. The incident I speak of is peculiar. It occurred in Chicago last July. A stationary balloon company called the Colon Gabriel Yon Company operated a large gas balloon out on Cottage Grove avenue, and one could make an ascension to the height of 1000 feet and back again for the sum of $2.50. With a party of friends I ascended to the limits of the rope. Up at that distance a splendid view of the city and the lake could be had for miles around. We spent an enjoyable half hour and then signaled to be drawn in. Somehow our signals didn't work, at least we weren't drawn in with any remarkable haste. We kept up this desultory signaling from our heavenly flag station, but with no avail. We tried the top of our voices separately, and then I suggested that we give a unanimous whoop for liberty. The result was the same. We leaned out, all four of us, fully half our length over the basket side and waved our arms. I imagine that we must have appeared to the pedestrian public much like a parcel of paper pin-wheels stuck to the side of the basket and revolving in the wind. Then we became resigned for awhile, and this feeling would have continued only that one of the party suggested the possibility of a cyclone and of us being blown out into the lake or falling maimed and bleeding to the streets below. The possibility of this started the pin-wheel operations again, and we simply wore ourselves out endeavoring to attract attention. After an hour and a half of torture we felt the tugging of the rope, and the downward trip began. When we came within hailing distance of the earth we began to announce our unwavering purpose of pounding the life out of the manager and whoever else we might reach. We also threatened an immediate suit for damages. At last we crawled out of the basket and danced belligerently about looking for satisfaction. The manager explained that the employes had struck for higher wages and refused to let us down until he should grant their demands. He had sent for police, and upon their arrival we were hauled in. It seems laughable enough now, but we were almost frantic up there for awhile."

[*27 January 1893, p. 7, no. 6*]

No. 67.

D reams are curious mental waverings, indeed," said Hiram Teuton, as he puffed a cigar in the Lindell. "Not only is it strange that the mind should wander always over the past when one is at rest, but also it is strange to note how short they are. In dreaming I have often covered a period of ten years in my early life, and grasped in a hazy manner the principal events of the entire time. Not long ago I began to study over the shortness of my morning nap and the number of dreams that entered into the space of sleeping. I have awoke in the morning, looked at my watch, and observing that it was still early turned over for a second nap. In a little while I would find myself awake and endeavoring to recall some dreams that had troubled my little doze. Then I would imagine that I had been sleeping too long, hastily look at my watch and find that I had been asleep only a few minutes, and sometimes only a minute. Yet in that short space I had fallen asleep, dreamed of a dozen different events and persons, apparently a long mental wandering, covering hours, had awoke and spent a few moments in retrospective thought, and all in the space of a minute. I see now that a dream is computed to be extra long when it last ten seconds, and that the duration of an ordinary dream is five seconds. These figures are taken from the writings of a German scientist who has made experiments in this line during the last year."

[*28 January 1893, p. 5, no. 5*]

No. 68.

I heard a remarkable story relative to poisonous wood," began Maximilian Wideman to a crowd of friends in the Laclede. "It comes from the Chickasaw Indian Nation, and I have reason to believe it. An old Indian chief, who was possessed of a venomous nature, took enmity against a younger warrior of the nation for some small occurrence in the tribal life. He carried his hatred through a series of years and events, scheming, no doubt, how to rid himself of the younger Indian, who was rather idolized by the young braves. Not long ago the tribe and the American residents of neighboring villages were startled by the story of the sudden death of the young chief, his squaw and several young braves who were the young chief's best friends. They were evidently poisoned, for they were seized after a feast of wild deer and died in the most intense agony. Indians are superstitious enough without having anything mysterious to occur, but with it wild speculation is the result. Everything in the witch art was suggested. The Government officers of the district, who investigated the matter, laid the crime at the door of the old chief, and subsequent discoveries proved them correct. The old chief had soaked bits of decayed wood in the gathered poison of a rattlesnake, and by some means had conveyed it into the broth of the cooked venison. A portion of the composition was found upon him. It was boiled with meat and fed to an

61

Indian dog, which, a little later on, died in apparent agony. From personal experience I want to add that anything that will kill an Indian dog will destroy life and soul also in a human being."

[*28 January 1893, p. 5, no. 6*]

No. 69.

See this pearl?" said Clifton Sparks to a *Globe-Democrat* reporter in the Laclede, as he held aloft to view a beautiful specimen from the sands of the Indian Sea and twirled the gold in which it was set to show off its superior value. "That pearl is worth $300 in the market to-day, but the circumstances under which it was discovered makes it invaluable to me. It's a gift from my mother, who received it from my father, and he got it for nothing. My father was a Captain in the English army and was stationed in India. On his homeward voyage, after a stay of twelve years in India, he accidentally acquired this pearl. He got it from a sea-gull, and the sea-gull from some pearl oyster that was washed up on the strand by the waves. My father fished for sea-gulls with a hook and a bit of bacon. He caught two gulls, and dissected them for his own amusement. In one he found this pearl, which, when he reached London, he had set in gold, and gave it to mother as a souvenir of the long ocean voyage. Acids are very deleterious to pearls, and when you con-

sider how perfect this one is you can imagine that the gull had not long swallowed it. I don't know of a similar instance, and that is why it is invaluable to me."

[*30 January 1893, p. 5, no. 4*]

No. 70.

Is there anything more blissful in all this world than that condition in which a man looks dreamily upward into a cloud of smoke and views the world through a pale hazy film?" said Oram Melvale as he did likewise in the Lindell. "We speak of viewing the world through a colored glass and making it look beautifully red and blue or green, but viewing it through smoke makes one not only see a richly-colored world, but also one in which evil is not contemplated and pain is forgotten. To me the smoke is half magic, for it makes the tiresome hotel corridors along my route fade into nothing. In their place it leaves a kind of an enchanted garden in which I linger in perfect rest. Friends come back and bring with their coming old days of sunshine and country scenery through which we used to travel together. Everything is warm, mellow, rich in its perfection, and then I feel as I imagine a man ought to feel were he perfectly successful and famous. I half believe in the old transmigration of souls theory when I think of it. Just imagine some soul living and growing in a tobacco plant, and being released only in the smoke of it. Can't you imagine that the smoke might be a thankful, blissful soul that lingers in the film over you and brings back beautiful visions? I confess such speculations all charm me into missing my train."

[*30 January 1893, p. 5, no. 5*]

No. 71.

"One of the most deceiving objects that I ever witnessed," said Roman Jordan, who is at the Southern, "is just outside the little town of Hester, Colo. It is a tree, some 40 feet tall, the first 20 feet of its height being a circumference of some 7 feet round. Twenty feet from the ground the tree suddenly narrows down to a circumference of some 4 feet. Upon examining it you would come to the conclusion that it was a freak of nature. It gives the impression that some one had sawed the upper half of the old tree off, and that instead of dying a smaller tree had grown up from the center. It is the object of much speculation and visits on the part of strangers, while the inhabitants blissfully hold their peace. The facts are that what appears to be one tree is really two. The great old tree of which the first 20 feet is the remaining relic was hollow, rotten at the heart. A great wind came some years ago and broke off the upper half, leaving a jagged pillar some 22 feet tall remaining. This hollow heart

was burnt out more than once by squirrel hunters who imagined that the game had entered into the tree through the aperture at the base. The wind must have blown an acorn down into this hollow center for a tree sprung up in it, and grew straight upward and out into the sunshine. For appearance sake the owner of the ground sawed off the jagged portion at the top, making it level and smooth. The young oak has flourished well until now it fills the heart of the tree very compactly. The opening at the base has been hidden by earth piled about, and also by wild ivy that is fast covering the stump. If no one explains the matter it simply leaves the stranger to figure out a ninth wonder."

[*30 January 1893, p. 5, no. 7*]

No. 72.

"The most wonderful exhibition of confidence by one person in another came before me a short while back on my tour through Germany," said S. C. Oldfather, who is at the Laclede. "I have a great deal of confidence in some men's ability, and a wonderful trust in some men's nerve and steady strength, but not enough to stake my life on either. The exhibition that I saw seemed foolhardy. It was in the works of the great Krupp Arms Company. One part of the machinery is for flattening bars of steel into plates. For this a special machine is had, which has an immense steel block or table on which to lay the bars, and a great arm sledge, which weighs several tons and comes down with crushing velocity. It is perfectly regulated by machinery, however, and the man at the throttle can stop it with ease at any given distance from the block, providing he have sufficient steadiness of nerve. The day I went through the manager accompanied us and requested the man at the check-valve to show us how sure and certain was the machinery. Without reply the mechanic whistled to a lad working some 30 feet away. The boy dropped what he was doing and came running. 'Jump up,' said the first, and muttered something about showing us the machine. Without reply the lad leaped to the steel table beneath the great iron blocks. We were horrified, but the work was too quickly done to permit objection. The moment the lad settled down the engineer grasped the lever and the great sledge with lightning rapidity flew up and down again toward the block. It was all done in a second. Its downward course was checked by the steady fingers at the valve, and it stopped a few inches above the lad's head, who smilingly climbed down and started away. We raised a purse to present the twain with, which was at first refused. The manager finally consented to order them to take the money, which they did. I never expect to witness such another exhibition of confidence and nerve."

[*31 January 1893, p. 7, no. 7*]

No. 73.

I know of an experiment made not long since in a French hospital which was decidedly novel and valuable, although it seems brutal," said Emerson Jennison, who is at the Lindell. "It has long been a matter of great difficulty to get anything like exact models of the interior of many of the human organs for educational purposes. One French professor hit upon a novel scheme. He wanted to get a model of a dog's stomach when in its ordinary condition. How to do this was a matter of serious reflection. He had seen models of many parts of a dog's anatomy, but never a model of the entire stomach and gastric channels in working order. Finally he thought of plaster of paris in a liquid condition. He immediately secured a small cur from the streets and killed it. Then by a series of knife punctures and the insertion of metal drains he cleared the stomach of all its contents. The next thing was to forcibly inject the fast thickening plaster which an attendant had prepared. After that the dog was laid away for several days. When it was again taken up and the flesh dexterously removed a perfect model of the entire intestinal system was left, which was later sent to the Academy of Science in Paris. The work was a revelation to many and will undoubtedly be productive of much good."

[*1 February 1893, p. 7, no. 4*]

No. 74.

S mall white hands for gentlemen may be pretty, they may be an indication, but to me they are only useful and interesting in one respect," said Franklin Kinsey, as he nervously trotted to and fro across the corridor of the Lindell. "That use is that they help me to keep away from the owners of them. When I see the hands I can tell whether or no I care for an introduction. I have visited the salons of the dilettanti of most of the great cities of the world, and I have found that small white hands on men are good danger signals. You can always tell the hand that has labored. It's a legacy of honor that nature sees fit to decorate a man with. I used to take pleasure in shaking the hand of every man, but the small white hand is cold. Its grasp is weak, and the action half-hearted. I have become a crank on the subject. I stroll through the halls of the rich where one finds gathered the elite, and search constantly for rough, large hands that some one is trying to conceal, nervously fidgeting with, not knowing what to do with them; they look of a sudden so large sticking out from clean white cuffs. When I have found them I have found pleasure for the evening. I have found some one who is broad and interesting, some one who can not talk on the little topics of the hour, but who lets slip now and then answers clear-cut and meaningful that chime ill with the surroundings, but well with the soul. I may be a cynic and a crank, but through forty years I have tried to disprove my early conviction and have utterly failed."
[*3 February 1893, p. 7, no. 2*]

No. 75.

I t is queer in what esteem, almost reverence, the stork is held by the populace, the common people, of Germany," said Harry Stone at the Lindell. "This bird, with its solemn, morose aspect, is considered a bird of good omen, and its location in the chimney tops of the lowly houses is always desirable. To me, in fact to most every American, the stalky lankness of the bird and the air of all-pervading wisdom and reflection suggested by the half-closed eye and the drowsy aspect of the bird in general is decidedly humorous. Children are forbidden to fling stones at them; inducements to settle are offered, such as the scattering of wheat kernels on the house top in the springtime, but sometimes these things are useless, for the bird does not come. If for any cause the bird should leave before the season's end it is looked upon as an evil omen, a dire portent of misfortune. I have had quite a number of good German country folk tell me of deaths and crop failures that have followed the birds' departure, and how the evil continued until by some good fortune the stork family was induced to return. Now all this is a kind of mythology, a kind of primeval worship, little higher than that of the Egyptians who worshiped the sacred ibis, and the Druids of England who bowed before stocks and stones. You will find this superstition in a hundred forms believed in by lowly peasants and by men of the deepest literary pursuits and reflection. It does seem as though every man's life is domineered by some guiding influence, whether it be a stork or a dead ancestor, and almost every man, deep down in his own consciousness half feels that something hangs over him — that something is leading him on."

[*3 February 1893, p. 7, no. 3*]

No. 76.

O ur music is as much a result of the process of evolution as we are," said Howard Mandeville to a *Globe-Democrat* reporter in the Laclede. "You can see what the music of 4000 years ago was if you listen to a Chinese band, or view the Chinese instruments. Their music, like their civilization, has not changed in that period of time, and they play to-day much as the old bards are supposed to have played while going through the religious rites prescribed by the code of Confucius. I once listened to a Chinese husband, unseen, I must admit, who, for fully an hour, dolefully extracted discords from a queer-shaped instrument, probably the great-great-grandfather of our modern violin,

much to the delight of the remaining members of the family. At first I thought that he was simply sounding the strings preparatory to tuning them, but when after certain marked periods he stopped and the family gave various grunts of approval I concluded that he had executed some delightful love ditty in Chinese. But music is really the product of a finished genius, whose education in that line began several hundred years before he was born. I observed a peculiar incident in the little town of Albion, Ala., that had, in addition to the city proper, a small suburb called 'Baptist Town,' where none but colored people lived. There were fully 500 of them, and they had a business quarter of their own, including a town hall. Some guiding prophet among them endeavored to collect the musical talent of the village together and organize a band. The organizing part of the scheme was successful and the band met every Wednesday and Friday in the evening. When I reached Albion the band had been in existence some seven years, but had never given a public entertainment. I wondered why until the first Wednesday night came. Then my wonder ceased. The band had a perfect organization, full uniforms, a band leader and all the facilities for improvement, yet improvement there was none. It was not in them. On these evenings they were wont to gather, and their gathering was interesting. From the various quarters of the little hamlet they issued from their homes, leisurely strolling toward the hall, playing as they went on their chosen instrument with a degree of perfection that was exasperating. The twilight hour, the still quiet streets and the responding sounds from some distant approaching comrade lent a charm to the situation that made up for the lack of harmony. In the hall the opening dash of the leader's baton was the signal for a grand discord, and so on until 11 p.m. It is such things as these that bear out my evolution theory."

[3 February 1893, p. 7, no. 5]

No. 77.

A person is occasionally placed in an embarrassing position when least expecting it," said B. J. Oswald, who is a guest of the Lindell. "Of all such occurrences the strangest yet in my experience was that of a female cousin of mine who went into a trance in my presence, and while in that condition repeated the words of some character that had spoken them several months before in a dream of mine. This, too, in the presence of the assembled household. It was a very common occurrence for me to spend the afternoon with her, playing duets as we did and singing together. Some four months previous I had a dream in which a girl whom I did not recognize, but whom I still called cousin, spoke to me telling me that I was going away and that there were certain obligations which I must fulfill be-

fore I left. I never paid any attention to the dream, however, until it was recalled by her words while in this trance. It was an afternoon in early spring—a warm, pleasant day—and we both sat in the parlor talking over one thing and another. I began talking about my future prospects and the hopes that I entertained respecting certain things. All at once, without the shadow of a warning, she reeled over to one side of her chair and lay perfectly still. I was scared considerably and lustily called for assistance. The other members of the family came, and it was then that she began to repeat in a wandering way the long-forgotten scene of my dream. I was astounded, and you can imagine that the others present were also. I was fearfully embarrassed. When she awoke we inquired what caused her to lose consciousness and repeated to her the words she had spoken. She remembered the language, but could not imagine why she should have used it. I said nothing until a few days later, when I told her of my dream. The whole thing seems inexplicable except that portions of the dream have come true, and I expect the other part to be fulfilled. Such things seem to indicate—I hardly know what."

[4 February 1893, p. 5, no. 3]

No. 78.

As much as I have studied the habits of the American crow," said Columbus C. Everett at the Lindell, "I never found anything disagreeable about him. I have often wondered where a crow gets its wonderful vision and power of scenting danger. They are queer birds, always looking down on one with an ominous eye, that bodes no friendship. I never realized what awful and evil intelligence these birds have until I studied another type of them, the raven of India. When I traveled in India, three years ago, I made many journeys on pack animals through long, dreary sections of territory. It was then that I perceived their wisdom. On more than one occasion our little party was followed for hours and days by ravens, a hungry swarm that kept a certain distance, but never lost sight of us. I began to wonder why we were shadowed by these hungry birds. Some of the natives said that they were watching for some of us to fall by the wayside. As an experiment I shot a dog and left it lying. These miserable vultures attacked it at once, within a stone's throw of us. I should wonder little but that the American crow has the same tendencies, and only awaits a scarcity of grain to show them."

[*8 February 1893, p. 7, no. 7*]

No. 79.

Why will a man die right at the threshold of his career?" asked Wesley Sisson, of New York, at the Lindell yesterday. "Here is Henry C. De Mille, a man whom I knew better than my brother, dies right as he is entering the door of success. Let me tell you something about De Mille. Nobody in the world knew him better than I did. He dies famous; I won't. Everything of late years that he touched his hand to turned to money. In former years nothing made money for him. There is a singular fatality in his death. James De Mille was a relative of his, and he, too, died on the threshold of his career. He was a novelist. He wrote 'Cord and Creese,' 'The Cryptogram,' 'The American Baron' and a number of others, and just when he was beginning to be known he died. Henry De Mille was like him in this. His writings the world knows by heart. His first effort, 'Delmar's Daughters' was a failure, not because of lack of merit, but through the jealousy of David Belasco. His later efforts, 'The Lost Paradise,' 'Men and Women,' 'The Charity Ball' and others have been big successes. Why? Because De Mille wrote for the people, and the people will remember him long after the profession has forgotten him. But my first question holds good, 'Why will a man die at the very threshold of his career?' "

[*13 February 1893, p. 5, no. 2*]

No. 80.

I noticed with keen enjoyment," said J. P. Edwards to a *Globe-Democrat* reporter, "a funny squib that some paper had started, and which went from one editor to another throughout the land, gaining with each journey a comical addition that added much to the idea. One said 'that the Sioux Indians had a newspaper of their own; delinquent subscribers will be promptly scalped.' Another added: 'No, this is wrong, they will be Siouxed.' A third said: 'Scalping subscribers would soon leave the editor in the siouxp.' A fourth said: 'The Sioux-ner the better.' A fifth added: 'Certainly if Sioux-table,' and a sixth soul worn with the hilarious outrageousness of the growth soliloquized: 'A much-worn and aggrieved American populace is now willing to *Sioux* for peace and relegate these comments as a Sioux-venir of the Sioux-preme ability of American editors to joke if they please.' "

[*17 February 1893, p. 7, no. 1*]

like the old Mosaic law, commands that no graven image, however distorted or feeble, shall be made of any coin, scrip or bond issued by the power of the realm. In accordance with the literal meaning of the law a great stew was brewed up in the City of Chicago over a painted figure of a $20 note. A local sign painter of that city contracted to paint on one of the many great sign-boards of that city an advertisement for a local money loan company. The artist painted a hand holding a great $20 note, fully 8 inches by 2 feet in size, and over it were the words, 'Do you need any money?' This went well enough until the Government agent of that city one day, strolling about, espied the sign, and forthwith ordered the painter to remove it. He also ordered the arrest of the said painter and ordered suit brought. But for once in a thousand, the spirit of the law was so apparent and the offense so justifiable that even a Chicago Judge was enabled to perceive it, and the unwitting offender went scot free."

[*17 February 1893, p. 7, no. 3*]

No. 81.

The letter of the law truly furnishes the queerest incidents that one may ever wish to hear of," remarked Wesley Lewis to a party gathered about in a chair circle in the Laclede. "The letter of the law that relates to counterfeit money is the richest of all. It,

No. 82.

People speak of companionship," said Oldfield Newman to a friend in the Lindell, "companionship of others, I mean. Now, I've often speculated on that term, and it seems wonderful in what countless variety one may find companionship outside of living friends, the power to infuse personality into everything about one. Riding in a railroad car I am ever enabled when alone to find solace in the click, click, click, click of the gliding wheels over the rails. Many a time I have lain drowsed, almost in dreamland, listening to this sound. I have made it rhyme to every tune that I ever knew. I have divided it into regular poetic feet, and made a certain click come with rhythmical cadence certain to chime in with some word that ought to fit into such a rhyme. At such times the sound of a human voice has been most harassing. I have found companionship in the dripping of the rain from the eaves of a roof, and again in the fall of the year when the brown leaves come down I have made their circling about, around and around as they came to earth, rhyme with my thoughts. It does seem as though there is some spirit in all these things that is full of friendship, of harmony, and is more than friends and words to one when reflecting still and alone."

[*17 February 1893, p. 7, no. 4*]

No. 83.

I maintain now, and trust that I always will, that bachelors are the broadest-minded men," said K. Loneman Bradfield to friends at the Laclede. "Not all bachelors are wide in their sympathies,

but there are those of them known as Bohemians who compose a class that typifies in a measure the ideal of a universal soul. I know that such a statement as this is usually productive of a whoop of contradictive recrimination, but now, I ask, isn't it so? These beings come together in a manner totally foreign to the meetings of men who wrapped themselves up in one affinity, incased themselves, oyster-like, in the shell of a home. These Bohemians discuss with loving freedom all that is beautiful along the varying pathways that lead from eternity to eternity, winding for a little distance their way across this earth of ours. Their love is a universal love, their longings universal longings. They look from without into the home, and sorrow that it may not be their own, and yet they feel the narrowness of it; all sorrow again that they are not narrow. Many of these men reflect that the women they might love would grieve that their sympathies should extend out and beyond the little home circle. They picture a heart wearing away with this sorrow, and, with a manliness that is again typical of universal strength, they forego their pleasure to spare the pain. I can not help but figure out that minds that find continual solace within the four walls of a home are home minds, and not universal as these others of which I speak."

[*17 February 1893, p. 7, no. 6*]

No. 84.

"When one speaks of love at first sight, boundless love and all that," began Walter T. Hale in the Lindell, "the ordinary listener is apt to reflect that some one has been reading cheap novels. I know of a case of love at first sight that is remarkable, and one that is as absolutely as it is strangely true. I had a friend. I only wish that that term meant to every one what it means to me. This friend was spoken of as cold, cynical, self-contained by nearly all who met him. The truth of it was that he was naturally buoyant and heart-warm, but was a prey constantly to a soul-corroding longing. Recollections of better things troubled him until he was unhappy, listless and aimless when not grieving. One night I took a picture from my pocket, that of a beautiful girl. A face that was serene in its beauty, youth and intellectual comprehension. He took it rather disinterestedly, but changed with the first glance. He held the face to the light, and began with pain-shadowed features to comment on its beauty. I knew her well, and he described without hesitation all the qualities that she so richly possessed. I had been the unhappy harbinger of pain. My friend's sensitive nature saw in this face an affinity that called out all his spiritual affection. He studied it time and again until his days were of constant longing. This wonderful passion lasted through years, and domineered his being in a most mar-velous manner. I doubt whether he has yet outgrown it. I must add that when I saw how his affection was eased and fed on hope I had not the heart to tell him that I, too, had adored this being and that she was dead."

[*17 February 1893, p. 7, no. 7*]

No. 85.

"You may talk of the ethical side of this earthly existence all you want to," remarked Austin D. Brennan to companions in the Southern, "but that side don't suit me at all. It seems that many people take especial delight in standing alone on what they consider their reason regardless of any precept or orthodox consideration of any kind. I believe that those people are wrong. The Lord didn't intend that a man should reason out everything. At least there are innumerable mysteries which no person has yet been able to comprehend, and until such mysteries as may be are clearly understood I think that no one can stand on a comprehension which does not comprehend. These believers in the right may be the same. They may have grasped the truth of existence, but for my part I would rather believe that these countless cohorts of Christians are more in touch with the Supreme Will than these latter progressists. I may not do exactly right, but if I have faith in a greater

71

benevolent Power, I do believe that I am happier than the man who has only his reason to depend on."

[*18 February 1893, p. 5, no. 1*]

What makes it pretty is that the young lady now wears that ring as a token of my esteem. She is my wife."

[*18 February 1893, p. 5, no. 3*]

No. 86.

I went bathing in Lake St. Clair, about three miles from Mount Clemens, Mich., and lost a ring," said Maxwell Appleton, who is at the Laclede. "Lake St. Clair makes a delicious bathing ground, for there are miles and miles of sandbars in it, not under 3 feet of water. I thought to watch my ring by keeping it on, but in the delight and excitement of the sport it slipped. It was engraven with my name and city, so that I had hopes of sometime seeing it again. An hour of search proved fruitless, and at last I gave up in disgust. The following summer of 1890, in the month of July, a polite note on tinted, perfumed paper came to me, announcing that ring with name had been found and could be had at ---- Gratiot avenue. I repaired to the residence and was greeted by an over-polite footman, who showed me the parlor and disappeared. A little later a fair young lady came down and brought with her the ring, which I received with my best acknowledgments. She had found it while bathing. The romantic side of it all conquered me. A little later I formed the desired acquaintance and spent a pleasant August with my new friend.

No. 87.

I had an interesting, I might say humorous, thing happen to me once while out fishing," said Odin Everett Tazwell, as he smoked in blissful leisure at the Lindell. "One afternoon a chance summer acquaintance of mine, up in Northern Wisconsin, strolled over to my boarding house and proposed that we go fishing for the afternoon. It was a warm day, and he spoke of a cool little island down the stream a bit which was all shaded with trees and carpeted with grass. The prospect seemed too good, so I got down 'Tom Jones' from the library, turned over a few sunken boards of the walk for fish worms, and then with a prospect of a grand combination of pleasurable reading, fishing and dozing, we started away for the stream. We paddled down the stream in a little dugout and finally landed. I settled myself comfortably on the grass with a small log — coat-covered — for a pillow, and prepared to do three things at once. I decorated my hook with an appetizing fish attracter, stuck my pole in the mud that it might support itself, and opened my novel. My friend settled down a little farther on with the single purpose of fishing.

Certainly that afternoon went pleasant. I followed the interesting fortunes of 'Tom,' watched with ticklish interest a suspicious nibble that disturbed the perfect calm of water about my cork, and occasionally inquired of my friend how they were coming. My cork never completely disappeared, however, and so I left it undisturbed. The afternoon waned and with the setting sun my companion pulled up stakes and came to say he was going. He had a fine string of fish and guyed my luck. I closed my book and pulled up my line. On my hook was a little 2-inch perch, that throughout the entire afternoon had deluded me with the idea that I was fishing. I was thankful to the fish, however, for I had with my reading the constant enjoyment of 'a bite.' "

[*18 February 1893, p. 5, no. 5*]

No. 88.

Y ou can't tell me anything about theatricals," said Paul Dunn, who is at the St. James. "I've been knocking about now for a number of years, and I feel confident of one or two things. Just wait until I get my airship patented; then you will see how a modern troupe ought to travel. I tell you I've got the comprehensive scheme. All the airship has got to do is to travel 200 miles a minute and then we could start. I would take my troupe and open in New York Monday night, play San Francisco Tuesday night, Buenos Ayres Wednesday night, Melbourne (Australia), Thursday night, Alexandria (Egypt), Friday night, London Saturday night, and finish the week in Chicago Sunday night. It's a great scheme. No lost time, no trouble dodging creditors, good health, appetite, and all that. I've got the scheme all planned out. Now all I need is the airship."

[*20 February 1893, p. 5, no. 2*]

No. 89.

T he prettiest sight that greets the eye in these occasional days of sunshine that come with the approach of spring," said Richard Hasick, who is at the Laclede, "is that of a little bunch of violets in the lapel of a gentleman's coat. There is nothing, I confess, that fills me with so much of buoyancy and joy as these little nosegays. The rich odor and the depth of their color contain all the visions of a long, warm summer time, with sunshine, birds and flowers. When I see with what pleasure men purchase violets now and their numerical increase day by day, I begin to feel as though human beings are much like plants, with a vitality that withdraws in the dull gray days of winter after the manner of the sap of trees. The first breath of warm air, the first morning of bright streaming sunlight brings them out, the vitality begins to flow upward into the heart and they bloom out in nosegays of violets and sprigs of all early plant life."

[*20 February 1893, p. 5, no. 3*]

No. 90.

It is a question just how far a silk hat and a supreme nerve will carry a man in this work-a-day world," said Harmon Ellis, who is at the Lindell, "but it looks as though the American public still succumbs with grace to such potent influences. The best instance of this is Col. Hale, of nowhere in particular, but who has a habit of blowing in with the spring breezes and promoting things general, much to his own interest. Col. Hale blew into a rapidly-growing Western town recently and quickly grasped the fact that there was no cable road. With everything gone but a silk hat and $125 he spent $100 for admission in a swell local club and proceeded to exist on the remaining $25. He gathered about him the leading moneyed men and laid bare the scheme of millions in a cable road. He agreed to obtain the franchise and put it all through for $30,000, part of which was to be paid down as a guarantee of good faith. Do you believe that that fellow dusted up his silk hat and attacked the Aldermen next? By dint of promising and pompous appearance of wealth he secured an ordinance, was voted stock, drew what was coming

to him and blew out again, leaving everyone to wonder."

[*20 February 1893, p. 5, no. 5*]

No. 91.

The term 'unconquerable feeling,' taken literally, is still an actual fact," said Ives Armford to a *Globe-Democrat* reporter in the Lindell. "There are times when feeling is the master, and strive as one may, it still holds, dictates and drives in a manner that is strangely supreme. Its dictation is inexorable, even in things most trivial; in things that it would seem a duty and a pleasure to do. I want to tell of one specific instance where feeling barred temporarily. One night somewhat over a year ago I decided to renovate my trunks. I get an unconquerable desire to renovate my trunks about once every six months, and nothing will do but that I must pile everything out, sort, cast aside, burn, and repack. On this night I began by laying everything out and then slowly to unfold bits of paper, letters, manuscripts, etc., seemingly without end. I only began at midnight and I was not done by 3 o'clock in the early morning. I picked up a letter from the disordered heap—a worn, faded sheet that I first thought to destroy. However, I opened it and took one glance. Then I dropped it. If ever I wanted to read anything in the world I wanted to read that letter, and yet I couldn't. After spending minutes in painful recollection I laid it, unread, into the trunk again. You wonder, no doubt, how a letter could bar my desire. It was from my dead mother, written to me months before when at school, and it seemed like a voice from out the great unknown, and I could not touch it."

[*20 February 1893, p. 5, no. 8*]

No. 92.

There is only one class of people that make good money in this land of ours or any other land," said W. R. Considine, who is at the Lindell. "That is the manufacturing class, and that class alone. I have spent a number of years in business in counsel, work and reflection, and I want to say once and emphatically to the aspiring young American, if you want to be successful and immensely wealthy you can do it only in one way, and that is to manufacture something — something that can be sold to wholesalers. Now just look at the country to-day. Who are the millionaries and people of influence? They are not the politicians, for all the boodle that there may be in it. They are not the theatrical class — managers, players or owners of theaters. They are not the real estate dealers, the merchant speculators nor the retailers. Neither are they newspaper men. They are by a rousing majority in every community the men who manufacture something — the pork packers, steelworkers, cloth-makers and the like,

and they have the best homes, easiest time, most respected families and everything they like in any community that you may enter. It comes right down to the simple fact that you can manufacture an article and charge very near what you please for it, up to 1000 per cent of its value. The way of the manufacturer is the way of success without a doubt."

[*21 February 1893, p. 7, no. 2*]

No. 93.

About a week ago," said Count Bozanti Chaipruski, Modjeska's husband, at the Southern yesterday, "we were in Winona, Wis. I went down to the station and told the agent there that I had some trunks I wanted him to check for Modjeska. He said all right, and took down a great big chart and commenced to study it. I waited a few minutes, and then, becoming impatient, I asked him why he did not check those trunks. The train would soon be along, and I was in a hurry. The fellow said he would check them in a moment, and started to study the chart again. Finally, putting it down, he said: 'I can't find that station; it's a new one to me; where is it?' 'What station?' I asked. 'Why,' he replied, 'Modjeska; it isn't on this chart, and I can't find out anything about it.' And yet we wonder why trains are wrecked."

[*22 February 1893, p. 7, no. 1*]

No. 94.

If a person but turn his eyes to his 'in'ards,' as I have heard one's vitals called," said Patton Rawsen, who is a Lindell guest, "that person is apt to draw much consolation from thence in times of trouble. Now, I was just reflecting that a man is never happy unless, in the current phraseology, he 'has a kick coming.' There is no use getting around it; one must recognize that dissatisfaction is the lever that moves the world. That man who has nothing to worry over has most. He has to grieve that his life is inane, useless, valueless. With satisfaction comes 'innocuous desuetude,' and, the Lord knows, to have that phrase flung at one is enough to make the dead roll over. I know a millionaire down in our section who kicked to himself over his business relations until he renounced them and retired. Then he grieved that he was retired. A very little thing seemed mountain high to him, I know, for most of the big things he could overcome with one bound, and it left him nothing but the little matters to quarrel with. I find that a man is most happy when he is preoccupied, and he is most preoccupied in work when endeavoring to surmount some obstacle that is a constant menace to his happiness."

[*22 February 1893, p. 7, no. 4*]

No. 95.

That is the most peculiar and astounding faculty of the mind that calls the new the beautiful," said Charles Truax, who is at the Lindell. "Now, just think a minute. Look at the change in fashions, and then you see it perfectly. The hat that you wore last season—the one with the stiff rim and soft crown—how nice and nobby it looked then. Now, when you tried it on again the other day, accidentally running across it in the locker—why, it looked hideous, didn't it? It's impossible to define why this is so. You can't say it is because the mind dislikes old things—some minds don't; nor that all minds love the new, the change. It isn't exactly because persons dislike to be odd or out of date, for some take great delight in looking strange and odd. Others do not wear the new things first simply to be the first. While I do not think this sense comes from or guides itself by any one of these influences, yet the sum of them all goes to make up a circle of harmony inside of which one would rather dwell than out. There are a thousand little things that the mind comprehends almost unconsciously and acts accordingly. It is this reflex action of brain work that makes it possible for one to understand why we do these things."

[*22 February 1893, p. 7, no. 5*]

No. 96.

I was out walking here the other morning," remarked W. Fairchild by way of introduction, as he strolled to and fro in the Lindell, "just to work up an appetite for breakfast. It was then beautiful — so much sunshine and warm air. In going out toward the suburbs I naturally passed through the meaner quarter of your city. Not very far out, in one of the poorer streets, I heard two women quarreling. I could not see them, but their voices were loud and shrill enough. The whole thing was a cloud or blot on the sunshine and the beauty of the hour. The voices increased in volume until one was fairly hoarse and snapping in its rage. Vile names and insinuations were thrown in a torrent of rage, and the beauty of the day seemed only to add to its seeming sacrilegiousness. Now, I thought of those voices so harsh and grating and then of another voice that I know — a woman's, too; a voice soft in its loving sympathy bending over the lonely, the weary and dying, breathing words of comfort in loving harmony; a voice capable of singing sweet low love tunes and uttering melodious words of cheer. The contrast struck me with such force that all my disgust turned to pity, and thinking of this — the better use — I felt that the sin must be fully rewarded in its committal."

[*22 February 1893, p. 7, no. 6*]

No. 97.

It is asserted by many," began Denton Trowbridge, who is at the Laclede, "that whatever ability a person has will certainly find a vent and find its level and proper environment regardless of adverse circumstances. Others again maintain that many a flower was born to blush unseen, etc., which may be equally true. But regardless of the truth of either, it is always interesting to note what exceedingly trivial occurrences often serve to develop some latent talent and declare to the sleeper for all time that he is indeed a man. A young fellow that I knew was for many — in fact all the years of his early home life — counted a lazy, stubborn, ambitionless fellow who was certainly doomed to the everlasting seclusion of ignorance and incompetence. He wouldn't study, work, obey nor do anything much but play one or two games of which he was very fond. With time, of course, he was sent out into the world. His habits changed. He became serious, earnest, conscientious and willing, but, lacking wofully in education, was compelled to do manual labor and waste his boyish spirit amid soul-killing influences. One thing after another was taken up with the hope of success, but to no purpose. Education was lacking, and many insinuated that even comprehension was not there. One day while in his miserable little room, tired from a day of drudge work, he exclaimed in almost an agony of despair, 'Oh, I'm losing heart. I want to die.' The exclamation was so sincere that the tears that followed were a mere matter of course. What struck me was the wonderful expression of his voice and the rich dramatic ease of his movements. I sat down and wrote a little speech from Richard III. I gave it to him and told him to study it and see if he could not give it dramatic expression by the following Wednesday night. When I came again he was prepared, and rising a little later he imitated to perfection the tiger-hearted descendant of the devil-king. I was pleased, but not astounded, at his wonderful ability. A few introductions to friends followed. Then parts in local dramatic exhibitions, and finally a course in a good dramatic school followed. He is as yet studying, but the world will shortly turn its eyes to a new tragic star, whose success will be as resplendent as it will be complete and rapid."

[*22 February 1893, p. 7, no. 7*]

No. 98.

There seems to be a growing opinion that whiskers are indicative of a foolish nature," said J. H. Compaire, who is at the Lindell. "The man with long, thin, wind-tossed whiskers is to the sturdy, smooth-shaven business man just what the jester was to the old-time king. Modern citizens look upon them as an inexhaustible source of humor, and the slightest allusion to the wind, accompanied by a feeling side glance and a passing of the hand across the chin, is ever provocative of a laugh. I don't think that the same sentiment holds good in regard to well-trimmed full beards and mustaches, nor, indeed, to any short, well-groomed hirsutal adornment, but the flowing kind—always. And oh, the names for them. Lilacs, celery, sea weeds, corn silk, midnight bells, hare-bells, windlets, and so on are mere suggestions of the list. The percolative dangulation of them at meal time will be a source of wit and jest. But great, long, thin whiskers, when it comes down to actual, hard sense, are neither adorning nor useful. To my mind, they are only illustrative of another way in which a man may make a conspicuous mark of himself."

[*23 February 1893, p. 7, no. 4*]

No. 99.

The financial downfall of any man should be the basis of sympathy for the poor devil that goes to the wall, but there are two kinds of failures in which sympathy is sadly misapplied," said Richard Saunders, of Boston, at the Lindell yesterday. "A man has been engaged in business for years and fails for $100,000. Then the business world speaks tenderly of him and offers its sympathy, and the general public is called upon to admire him. That same man has never done an act of kindness to any human being in his life. He has been a hard, unbending employer, and utterly devoid of the social instinct. He has obtained from his business friends $100,000, he has used it expecting to get more, he has given no equivalent for it and he fails. Yet it is all right; it was a legitimate business transaction and they are sorry for him. Take another case, in which sympathy is withheld. A man not in business fails for a paltry $100. What does the world say of him? That he is a beat, a cheat and a rascal, although he is a man of brains and is constantly striving to realize on his uncertain capital. He owes his tailor and his restaurateur, and means to pay them with the first money he gets. He dies. He owes $100 at the time of his death, and then his memory is denounced. Yet they will sympathize with the man who failed for $100,000 and never performed a kindness, while at the same time they have nothing but reproach for the man who paid his debts when he could and spent his money like a prince when he had it. There are two cases of misapplied sympathy for you."

[*23 February 1893, p. 7, no. 6*]

No. 100.

"The world laughs at the fool who, sticking his finger in a pool of water, withdraws it expecting to see a hole remaining," said Al Van Dyke, who is at the La-clede. "The same condition probably applies to air, yet certain things can be drawn through the air with such rapidity that a vacuum, which would correspond to the hole in the water, is formed. If not an exact vacuum, it is yet an almost vacant space into which the air rushes with great force. I thought of this last week while watching a passenger train going from Fort Wayne to Chicago over a fine roadbed. The train made splendid time, and left in its wake a cloud of dust that included sand, pebbles, straws and most everything else along the way. Where I stood there was a flock of geese picking along the track. The swift approach of the train disturbed them little, and the sound of the whistle was little better than Greek. They did not comprehend it. In a few seconds the engine was upon them. A unanimous flapping of wings followed and they made great efforts to escape. The truth is that they did escape from off the track, but the draught made by the rapid movement sucked the entire flock back under the wheels again. Nearly all were killed. One or two escaped the wheels, but they were drawn after the rear end of the train for fully 50 feet by the force of the suction. They were perfectly helpless, and fell to the ground with a thud when the force had passed over. I never clearly realized how much drawing power a moving train really had."

[*23 February 1893, p. 7, no. 7*]

No. 101.

I was just watching a negro that passed by here a few minutes ago with a dog tied to a string," said Christian Banks to a *Globe-Democrat* reporter at the Lindell. "If there is anything that is really humorous, it is to see a negro affectionately leading a dog that hasn't any affection for him at all, and don't want to have either. The garb was, as usual, indicative of the fact that the negro had little else to do except to take care of the dog. His hands were almost hidden by the length of his coat sleeves, and the coat itself hung in rich heavy folds over the shoulders and back in a manner more comfortable than graceful. The pants looked like segmented cloth-rings, piled one on top of the other from the ground up. They must have been warm. And there was that poor unpedigreed purp slouching along after in an humble, respectful way that was, however, only measured by the length of the string and the strength and toughness of it. Occasional jerks on the cord that pulled the dog's neck skin nearly over its head, and a 'come along, now, doan you go foolin' wif me,' indicated to the obedient animal that it was expedient to move along in this world. I just wonder now what a poor negro wants with a lean, lank dog. It's the old proverb over and over again, 'Misery loves company.' "

[*24 February 1893, p. 7, no. 1*]

No. 102.

The queerest of all ghost stories that ever I listened to was told to me from the top of an apple barrel up in Kennebunk Port, Me.," said P. Hemingway to a *Globe-Democrat* reporter. "An old salt who was possessed of a rather glowing imagination sat one evening in one of the general country stores and related the tale of the 'Ghost of the Rushing Wind.' It was of an old Indian hamlet and a log cabin, with a great brick fireplace. It was the only spot revisited by the spirit of some departed under the guise of a sobbing, moaning wind. The wind forever grieved alone in this great fireplace, when outside the night might be still and calm, and with the stars as clear and serene as ever they were to watching eyes at midnight. Nightly at 12, whether in an awful storm or perfect calm, whether cold or cool or warm, the wind came, rushing, whining, whirling always up the great chimney mouth, but forever confined until the shadows began to fade and morning was heralded by the earliest twitter of the birds. It was related that a trapper of ascetic nature had occupied the hut, and that one night, when probably discouraged by the loneliness of his existence, saddened by the reflection over joys long since dead, he had taken his life with the same trusty weapon that had been his only solace during years of hermit life. A dreadful storm held sway at the time, and ever as the hour of his death recurred, the ghost of the rushing wind returned to moan alone in the great fireplace much as it must have done at that fearful hour."

[*24 February 1893, p. 7, no. 2*]

No. 103.

A man's mind is like a camera. Now, isn't it?" queried Charles T. Rainbrook, who is at the Laclede. "I was just thinking to-day of this peculiar characteristic of the brain. It came about from the fact that I met here in the hotel an old friend whom I had not seen for years. My feelings were most pleasant, for he was an old companion of my youth. We lived side by side in a little country village, went to school together, played truant, fished, swam and skated together on a hundred different occasions. The fact is that we were much alike in our sympathies at that time. Now, I venture to say that had we both remained residents of that small village, receiving the same impressions from our environment, we would always have remained friends, always enjoyed the companionship of one another. But he went South and I went West. Undoubtedly we both found that human nature is very harassing in some parts of the Union, and the influences that came upon us varied greatly. The sum of all these years of worldly experience appeared in the glance of greeting that we gave one another. We were very far apart indeed. The gayly painted crafts in

which we set sail had changed, were weather-beaten and old, and rather unpleasant to look upon. So it came about that we probably parted with pleasure. I was saying, though, that the human mind was like a camera. That is, my friend was indelibly imaged upon my brain just as he appeared when last I saw him. My friend is still the same. I do not know this stranger at all, nor do I care to."

[*24 February 1893, p. 7, no. 3*]

No. 104.

I do believe," said Bronson Evarts to a friend in the Lindell, "that whisky will make anything drunk. The latest experience that I have had in that line was with an oyster bed that I have down in Chesapeake Bay. I have seen cats betrayed of their growth by whisky and dogs kept small. I have seen talkative poll-parrots bowled up until they fell off their perch and lay squawking and ha-ha-ing at the bottom of their cage in a most delirious manner, but I never saw an oyster bowl up except in restaurants, and then the oyster didn't know it. Down in Maryland I resolved to see what effect whisky would have on a small bed that I had for my personal use. I got some malt whisky one morning and went down to the bed. I let in fresh water and then poured in a little whisky. Next day I did the same thing, only I used more whisky. The whisky told on those oysters in a minute. It was too much for their nervous system. Whenever you touch an oyster's shell it closes up mighty quick and tight. I saw one lolling partly open and I put down my finger to touch it. It feebly closed up and then opened again. I tried it several times with the same effect. The oyster was not dead; it was simply too drunk to know that there was anything dangerous in this world. This condition lasted several hours, when the oysters would regain their wisdom and close up tight at the slightest disturbance of the water. I thought at the time of eating them that they had a peculiarly delicious flavor, but maybe it was because I was prejudiced in their favor."

[*24 February 1893, p. 7, no. 4*]

No. 105.

There are two gentlemen over there discussing the general uselessness of a person who can not quit any habit, such as smoking, chewing, drinking and the like," said Simon L. O'Donavan to a *Globe-Democrat* reporter. "If there is one thing more than another that appears to me pure bosh it is that one thing of talking about how easy it is to quit. It is the purposeless, shiftless man that can quit these things much easier than the man who has great force of character. Everybody admits that sternness of purpose, enthusiasm, animal fire and all that go to make the successful man — the man who makes a run and jump and

lands in first place. But no one ever had a purpose unless its accomplishment was graven on his very heart. It follows that his heart was susceptible to receiving a deep and lasting engraving. This very condition permits of some habit coming in and engraving itself on such a courageous yet susceptible nature; and once there it will remain as long as purpose remains and die when ambition dies. The man who can quit is the man who never smoked with any enjoyment anyhow, and who drank in a half tasting manner that boded nothing for himself nor any one else. So it is with his work; no great purpose ever stirred him and never will. He is simply lukewarm through life and dies the same way. When they talk of quitting they merely talk of giving up what interests them little, and then they stand about and moralize upon the weakness of human natures that can not give up pleasure. These same natures could surpass them at every turn in accomplishing a purpose, which they would relax after a little struggle with the same ease as they did their various habits."

[*24 February 1893, p. 7, no. 6*]

No. 106.

Really the most remarkable sight that I ever witnessed was about two weeks ago in the State of Pennsylvania," said Harry Oram to a group in the Laclede. "It was on one of the little lakes near Redville. Some men were cutting ice and storing it in a small ice-house that stood near by. The operations were conducted with the aid of two mules. While I stood watching the work one of the mules, traveling along very sturdily, suddenly stepped on a portion of weak ice. There was a sound of crunching, cracking ice, and the mule disappeared below. A cry of horror went up as the animal went down, for it was observed that it did not come up at the same place, and no doubt was held under by the ice. Amid the general wail, which lasted a minute and a half, the mule's head appeared above the water about 80 feet east where the ice had all been cut out. A grand rush was made, and by rapid adjustment of a rope the animal was towed to where it could stand on the sand. Later planks were put down and the mule taken out. But the remarkable thing was that that mule had swam 80 feet under ice and lived. Talk about mulishness!"

[*27 February 1893, p. 5, no. 1*]

No. 107.

I t's wonderful to think how much humanity hangs on environment," said George T. Marble, who is at the Laclede. "Human nature finds its level in luxurious surroundings always. There are, of course, persons who have seen their every wish and aspiration cast down and derided, who have been compelled to endure privation so long that they learn to do without and even to despise the beautiful comfort which wealth affords in this world, but this class is small. The great majority, though they may never attain the height of their ambition, never lose the sense of appreciation for it wherever it may be. Every one likes to look upon rich, heavy trappings in home and office, marble and mahogany, heavy plates, damasks and laces. Finished in metals even of gold and silver is ideal, but not beyond them. When one can not have all these he takes the next and makes the best of it. People may talk all they want about not wanting these things, and of the possessing of them making the soul narrow, but I believe the soul is more narrow without than with them, and that it is not refining by a long throw to be poor. I know of a certain environment that constantly gave one person the blues, and of another that worked upon a certain nature until it was driven to despair and committed suicide. Such occurrences as these are simply the opposite pole to that of self-abnegation. But, nevertheless, to my mind the grandest and most luxurious environment is the natural one."

[*27 February 1893, p. 5, no. 5*]

83

No. 108.

I've just been musing over the past," said Quinn Claremont, who is stopping a day at the Lindell. "Just thinking over the way we boys used to go swimming up in Michigan, and it does seem wonderfully amusing now. I remember one morning I awoke and saw the sunlight streaming through the window across my couch. Then I couldn't rest. I got up and stuck my head out. It was just pleasantly warm, but the pouring sunbeams promised a glorious hot day. Over the way I spied my game companion, Mick McConnell, pulling weeds in his father's garden. I pitied Mick, because his father had a garden and my father didn't. I hailed him just to show him that I was aristocratic and didn't have to work. Mick looked up and hailed in return. 'I say,' he said, 'let's go swimming.' That caught me exactly, and I decided that for one day I was just going to go and swim as much as I wanted to. When 9 o'clock came and the sun was getting dreadfully warm Mick eased up and went in to say that he ought to get off now until evening. Then we beat about the fences and made good our escape. There was one day that I will always remember. The water was fine and I staid in all the forenoon until I got hungry. I grieved to think that I had a stomach at all. As luck would have it I met the Jones boy, who wanted to go swimming, but not alone, and so I ate at his house and went back. This lasted, with proper mud-slinging, until dark. Going along the road toward home at dusk my rather drooping spirits were cheered by a convivial hubbub farther up the road. Another crowd was going. I met them. Their spirits were high, and with little effort this hilarious influence brought to me the mature reflection that perhaps I had misled myself into the belief that I had had enough swimming for one day. I gave in and returned. About 4,000,000 mosquitoes accompanied us. Something like 3,999,999 must have delighted in my company. That night I interviewed my father on various timely topics and retired sore and weary. Retribution came with a blistered back, plasters, rheumatism and water-itch. I think the scale weighed heaviest though on the swimming side."

[*27 February 1893, p. 5, no. 6*]

No. 109.

Who said evil is its own reward?" began Washington Lied, as he surveyed a crowd of friends in the Lindell. "Well, maybe that is true. The most peculiar occurrence in the way of swift retribution that I ever heard of or witnessed occurred right in my own home. It came to a cat of mine that much preferred to investigate the cupboard realm than to eat anything gratuitously given. This cat would prowl about from shelf to shelf, stepping in various articles of more or less fluidity, and leaving a trail of disaster that was enough to blight the ambitions of a stone-hearted cook. One evening, after supper was over, and this same cat had been properly feasted, there was a terrific explosion in the regions of the basement, and the servant immediately exclaimed, 'Oh, that cat.' We adjourned to the basement. Lights were brought, and we gazed upon the scene of destruction. In one corner lay our pet cat, close to the wall, as dead as a smelt. In the center of the floor lay a shattered can of blackberries that my wife had put up the season before for winter use. It was awfully plain. The blackberries had gone off with deadly effect. The cat had upset the can and then jumped, simultaneously with the can's falling, no doubt, for it received the full effect of the explosion and was blown into eternity. Since then I have taken great pains to illustrate to my wife the superiority of ready canned goods on the market. When we open one now we always send the cook about 20 yards from the house with it and hold our breath until she returns."

[*28 February 1893, p. 7, no. 5*]

No. 110.

I stood, not many months ago," said Ormes Landes, who is at the Lindell, "before the sacred temple in Mecca, close to the blessed Caaba, and saw the weary pilgrims bend to kiss the sacred stone. Now, if there is one thing more than another that is illustrative of the depths of the human heart, it is the sight of these Arabs bending over a stone. With what soulful reverence and humility they bent low and completed the aim of their life is far above any descriptive power that I may have. In seeing the jaded, footsore pedestrians walk seven times around the temple I conjured up the vision of their far-away Arabian home, and of the long, long journey across the plains and deserts to that queer old city, with its mosque temple and age-blackened relic. I thought then, 'now here is the turning point in their lives. All before this was the one great hope of completing a pilgrimage to Mecca and to receiving assurance of heaven. All beyond this is now a journey to the grave. With the faithful there is no other great earthly ambition to accomplish.' It illustrated to me the glory of even frail human strength which could so crystallize itself, year after year, about one thought, one hope, one deed, and after all these years of struggle find itself on the wane, yet able in the evening of life to wander into the sacred city and kiss the stone of life—the goal of ambition. There are inspiringly tragic scenes occurring daily in this great world of ours—little occurrences that mark the turn—but Mecca is one where a whole race and religion finds expression in accomplishing the most inspiring spectacle which the world ever has or ever will be called upon to witness."

[*28 February 1893, p. 7, no. 6*]

No. 111.

"The morality of this age is rapidly nearing the climax of degradation," began Rev. J. B. Lenivill, who is at the Laclede. "It must be a dull perception indeed that does not perceive the trend of the times. You see it on every hand — in literature, music, art and in fact, everywhere. The trend is towards the realistic and the luxurious. Just now the world seems to have an insatiable propensity for the exciting — change. It wants something new every day, and all precincts are invaded to obtain it. Nothing is too sacred. The downward evolution has seized our literature — it must be swift, short and spicy in plot. It must be a craving for the sensual and the luxurious. The stage has joined in the mad race. French plays are called for; something suggestive of the immoral. People want to go just as near the verge of moral degradation as they can and draw back unsoiled, to laugh at their own daring. The press has followed, and the most popular journals mirror this fast life in the clearest and most artistic manner. Men of business instinct now see the way to success and pander to this craving. The world shall have anything for money, and its every vice shall be lauded so that it pays for it and makes a ready market. The churches and homes are much more luxurious than religious. People won't do anything unless they can do it without effort. Society finds pleasure in discussing with grace and jeweled language subjects that between man and man, or woman and woman, would be considered immoral, and, as such, dropped. Yet young men and young women in company handle the themes with silk gloves, and their skill in so doing pleases them, for it is so exciting and so near the fall. It will go on, though, until every heart shall be satisfied and every desire of society cloyed. Then the reformation will come, and he that shall sing most lofty song shall again occupy the pedestal, and at his feet a world in sackcloth and ashes will bow in humility and sorrow."

[*28 February 1893, p. 7, no. 7*]

No. 112.

"There is only one way to obtain undying fame," said Wicklyff Bates, who is at the Laclede. "That is to write something. People who write, providing they write well enough, are sure of eternal fame. It isn't so with statesmen, generals, kings, or priests. Some of these live through the writer, but only as a subordinate character. Everybody recognizes and feels constantly while reading that the writer might have chosen any other character and written as well. So it makes one feel that the character chosen is simply a protégé of the author. The writings that live longest are those that advance a new solution of human motives and actions and state plainly and simply which is which regarding right and wrong. There is always a chance for some great mind to come along with this solution in language and character suited to the immediate conditions. It grieves pretty near every one to think that with them dies their name."

[*3 March 1893, p. 7, no. 1*]

just as cold as ever. Now, if heat can pass through cold glass without being affected, I do not wonder that it passes through limitless space of intense cold, and is still warm."

[*3 March 1893, p. 7, no. 2*]

No. 113.

I t is a subject of wonder to many, including myself," said Spencer Harding, who is at the Lindell, "that rays of light and heat should pass through intense darkness and cold and still retain their primal conditions of brightness and warmth. Some go even so far as to refuse to believe it, and maintain that light and heat of night and day and the seasons are the products of this earth, coming about from certain chemical combinations of the earth's own forming. It is just this end that I was thinking of, for if the latter is true then some one will have to explain why sunlight, passing through panes of glass, will warm the carpet on the floor, or, indeed, any other object lying in the light, while the glass remains perfectly cold. This is not due to outside conditions of weather at all, for it is the same winter or summer. You can hold a piece of glass inside a warm room, and back from the window a little, and although the sunlight may shine through it and heat up objects on the other side, yet the class will remain

No. 114.

C amera fiends are everywhere nowadays," said Stanton Thoop, who is at the Lindell. "I meet them wherever I go, climbing mountains, strolling through the cities, country towns and villages. They are in Europe, Asia, Africa and the South Sea Islands. When a man gets the camera wheel he is in one of the stages of insanity. Why, not long ago I came upon a party of pleasure seekers who were traveling anywhere that time and circumstance suggested. Two of them possessed cameras, and all of them had bicycles. I made their acquaintance and accompanied them for most a week on this desultory tour. One afternoon one of the members brought in the intelligence that he had discovered a gypsy camp some eight miles away and that they were just breaking up, preparatory to moving. The idea of a gypsy camp breaking up struck the camera fiends as a fine opportunity for a snap shot. What was to be done? — eight miles away and breaking up. They grabbed their cameras and, mounting their wheels, sped away like mad for the camp. In their lunatic chase one broke his wheel, the other his camera, but the man with the sound wheel took the good camera and kept up the good work. The other returned somewhat crestfallen bearing the wreckage. About dusk the first returned with a measly little plate of a band of departing gypsies, a better one than which can be bought any day for 10¢."

[*3 March 1893, p. 7, no. 4*]

No. 115.

I t's very humorous for one to revisit his native place after years," said Odell T. Kinsley, who is at one of the hotels, "especially if one has attained any degree of success. Of course this only works in a very small village where one is very well known. I'm not any more successful than a hundred other young fellows who come to the city from little, way-back points in the State of Ohio. Not long ago I went back to my native hamlet. My coming was advertised by relatives and a society squib in the local paper. It was announced that I was the city editor of the ----, and it was a very taking announcement. The following morning after my arrival I strolled out for a bracer and a shave. Everyone greeted me. I went into the bar and some half dozen old acquaintances shook hands and then sidled off and surveyed me in an awe-struck manner. 'He be the city editor of the ----' and 'He be a editor' were two

expressions that I caught at every turn. I went into the little barber shop and a dozen old friends who knew me when I was a kid 'accidentally' dropped in. I must have peculiar whiskers. After a few days the then admiring crowd took a reminiscent turn and I was regaled with tales of my 'queerness' as a boy. 'Allus wuz something funny about me.' Nobody'd ever thought that I would grow an' be a editor. You talk about enjoyment. A city never made a man so small but what a country village could make a giant of him still."

[*3 March 1893, p. 7, no. 5*]

No. 116.

H alf of the mysterious occurrences that we read about," said Henry Worthington, in the Laclede, "are mere conditions of nature that are rather recurring than continuous. People relate tales of strange lights and of death that follows, and of specters that appear once and are forever gone. I have found that certain localities have more of such literature than others. You can go into one community and hear an abundance of mysterious tales, whereas another district will furnish none or scarcely none. It all depends upon the intellectual status of the community and the density of population. A sparsely settled district in Russia or any of the more barbaric nations will furnish unlimited food for an author who prefers weird tales. The thickly populated districts and cities furnish a few, but not by educated residents. They are hearsay tales and come from the traveler. Certain portions of the earth are afflicted with a great falling of meteors throughout the year. Wherever these stone showers are frequent you can pick up innumerable tales of dragons, flying devils, demon lights and what not. In Northern Wisconsin, among the more ignorant Swedes, the falling of a meteor into a graveyard at midnight set the community by the ears until some disinterested geologist found a 14-pound meteor just where the fiery spook was supposed to have disappeared. In fact, ignorance is the only visible devil, but it is a specter that prowls about day and night in a thousand forms, forever able to scare the world out of its boots."

[*4 March 1893, p. 5, no. 3*]

No. 117.

"Making a pet out of a plant sounds queer," said Leif Manwarring to a *Globe-Democrat* reporter in the Lindell, "but I have seen a pet plant, and was the humble instrument of making it so. I sailed from San Francisco to Buenos Ayres around Cape Horn in a lumberman some ten years ago. The journey was of necessity and I did not anticipate much of a pleasant journey. By some odd fancy directed, after taking a delicious peach on the

day of my departure, I went and bought a small flower pot, filled it with earth and planted my peach seed. Then I went on board. I stowed my garden away and awaited developments. After some weeks of journey my peach tree put in an appearance and grew nicely in the warm atmosphere. There wasn't another sprig of plant life on board and when I showed my plant to the captain he called the crew and had them survey it. It seemed somehow to strike a homely chord of sympathy in them, for they went into affectionate ecstasy over it, and if anything more than sunlight and water had been needed, the plant would have been killed by kindness. Every morning of that long, long journey my peach tree was the source of grave solicitation, and many of the wise old wags laid their heads together in all seriousness to felicitate the best interests of the tree. It grew handsomely, and when we reached Buenos Ayres there came much sorrowing over the prospect of the loss of the plant. My sea journey ended there, and before I left the ship I presented the captain with the tree. This course gave immense satisfaction to all on board. Since then I have often wondered what became of my tree, but I have never met any of the old crew since."

[*4 March 1893, p. 5, no. 5*]

No. 118.

"A person can nurse a grievance of any kind with such constancy that it will become a mania," said Marshall Harriman, who is at the Lindell. "The present kindly term for such a condition is 'wheels.' If a man is a crank on no more than one thing he simply has one wheel and so on. I don't think wheels are objectionable, and certainly some of them are very entertaining. Most men with a fixed purpose in view and considerable strength of character have a wheel or two. The formation of wheels, or rather their growth, is what has always interested me. They are most noticeable in young persons, because they are brought out with more energy and enthusiasm than older persons could possibly rake up for their pets. A young fellow has a lurking suspicion that he can do something better than most any one else on earth, but is bashful and self-contained. This is a concealed wheel. Then he runs into a friend some day—a bright congenial—and, between these two, at least, bashful concealment evaporates. Then the wheel modestly puts in an appearance. It is well received, of course, and the friend soon finds that it turns with ease in his presence and is fast growing self-assertive. This gentle nursing gives the wheel great velocity, and it is impossible to keep it from turning in the presence of just moderate friends. Then any chance acquaintance is compelled to enjoy its gyrations, at which stage it becomes a nuisance and a fully developed wheel with noisy, grating cogs. There are poetic wheels, prose wheels, wheels of art, science and everything else. The most rampant of them all is the poetic wheel. We can thank friendship for all the blasted cranks who go about with an entire clock in their heads."

[*4 March 1893, p. 5, no. 6*]

No. 119.

"You have undoubtedly read now and again in the daily newspapers accounts of persons lying in a trance," said Frank Groniger, who is at the Lindell. "I am one of those persons. It is very harrowing to me to read accounts of people lying in this condition and being put in a coffin and even stored in a vault before they came to. I have even read of where, a few weeks after, some necessity caused disinterment and then the body was found turned face down, as though there had been a struggle for freedom. My experience went no farther than fifteen hours, I am certain, but that was enough, thank you. The fact is, I awoke one morning in my room feeling quite rested. I know that I had spent a pleasant night in sleep, and I lay speculating without moving or caring to open my eyes. Then I thought of getting up. I felt rather chill, I thought, but still comfortable. When I wanted to open my eyes I couldn't. When I tried to put my hands to them I didn't move. Then I struggled to stir at all, but it was only mental struggle. I then devoted my entire faculties to myself. I tried to call, but couldn't. My mind actually seemed to be ready to burst with rushing blood and confused thought. Then a relapse came, and I felt stupefied. I didn't care whether I moved or not. Then came alternate periods of mental struggle and stupor. In the afternoon I was discovered by my landlady, who came to look after the room. It seemed astounding to me to think that I should be compelled to lay there and appear as one dead. I heard everything that went on; heard her calls but couldn't answer. She called others of the family and a doctor. Burning my fingers and feathering my nose didn't disturb me. I couldn't feel it. I came around about 10 p.m. that night. When I did I came with a bound, and I was nervous for a week after. The thought of that probably coming again is a constant source of worry to me."

[*4 March 1893, p. 5, no. 7*]

No. 120.

I'm not a fatalist," said T. Davitt Henning, who is at the Lindell, "but occasionally I run across things that puzzle a great deal. Not long ago Dr. Tom Hewitt, of Leadville, Colo., died. Hewitt was somewhat of a fatalist, and believed in a great many things that I didn't. Omens and harbingers of evil he was much given to believe in. You have undoubtedly heard stories of people dying and the clock stopping at the same time, or some numerical of its face popping out. Hewitt had a sign in his office window in his residence which read: 'Dr. Tom Hewitt.' It was composed of eleven white letters glued to the pane. Hewitt took sick about sixteen months since. A few days after his illness I noticed that one of the white letters had dropped off and was gone. The illness of the Doctor caused the family to forget most everything else, and so the letter was not replaced. A month later Hewitt was still sick, and I noticed a second letter was gone. He lingered along, up and around now, and then sick again, for a period. Meantime the white letters were not replaced. Month after month went by, and every succeeding month saw a letter disappear. Hewitt noticed it, and then he would not allow them to be replaced. After ten months of illness, and when ten of the letters had disappeared, Dr. Tom got an extra severe spell of illness and died. The morning after his death I visited the house, and noticed, as I passed in, that the last letter was gone."

[*6 March 1893, p. 5, no. 3*]

No. 121.

A man never realizes how much of everything is stored up in the human mind until he begins to draw on it for a continuous period of time," said Marvin Temple, who is at the Lindell. "And then two things come back to one when entirely forgotten, and one really imagines that now here is something new and original until one learns better. This is especially true with old songs. Airs that at one time filled in moments of loneliness and gloom, but with a hundred other little details have long since passed out of mind, return. One stops and wonders at the beauty of them, and not having heard them before, according to memory, one takes credit for originality. I did this once. One morning I awoke with something pretty running through my brain. I framed in my mind a jingle and I could hear it just as plain, but to save me I could not give it sound. Finally after fretting about an hour and having completed my toilet I sat down before the fire and began to rock. Then all at once the power came and I hummed my new air over and over again with extreme delight. Visiting an old chum that evening I brought up the subject of music. Then I whistled my new tune and asked him if he did not think it pretty. 'I like that tune especially because my sister, who has been dead some thirteen years, sang it for me when I was still a schoolboy.' I eyed him with astonishment. 'You never heard that before,' I said. 'Why, that's original.' 'Original nothing,' came the rejoinder. 'I've got the piece in my trunk.' And sure enough, after rummaging through a great stack of useless treasure, he produced a faded piece of sheet music, my very tune, and with words to it. Then I gave myself up to reflection and eventually recalled the song as I had known it years before. Since then I have never trusted these new airs that come to me as pretentious originals — never."

[*6 March 1893, p. 5, no. 4*]

No. 122.

I never knew what an ascetic was really like," said the Rev. Father Burke, who is at the Laclede, "until some years ago. I had made an especial study of the lives of many of the characters of the dark ages, but I imagined that that sense of personal unworthiness was much less frequent in these days than formerly, and it undoubtedly is. I perhaps had better say that I never found my ideal ascetic until I met the Rev. Emanuel Weniger, a highly accomplished German and a Jesuit. This man was very famous as a Catholic missionary, and since his death his name has been prominent as fit for canonization. Some eight years ago I was pastor of a congregation in Southern Indiana, and while there I received word from the diocesan Bishop that a missionary would shortly be sent me. Late in the fall of the year, one very chilly midnight, a knock came at my door, and I arose and opened it. Outside in the shadow a man was standing. Without answering my greeting the person demanded the key to the church, which he took and disappeared through the shadow. Rather astonished, I dressed, and, taking a lantern, followed him across the field to the church. When I came he had been at his prayers several minutes. He knelt before the altar bolt upright, with his arms stretched upward to heaven in silent prayer. My entrance did not disturb him, and, kneeling down in a rear bench, I resolved to await the finish of his devotions. He prayed in that attitude until daylight. My later conversation with him developed the fact that he was Father Weninger, the famous orator and ascetic. His life was one of constant self-imposed tribulation. He endured unnecessary hunger, cold and thirst. He avoided companionship, and indeed everything that might divert his mind from his continuous thought of the future realm. This man inspired by his earnestness every one that he met, and so accomplished wonders in the way of conversions. I rather count this a kind of abnormal condition, though, and it is rather a consequence of birth than of intellectual study."

[*6 March 1893, p. 5, no. 5*]

No. 123.

I have had an experience that very few sensible persons have had," said John T. Shayne, who is at the Lindell, "and that is the experience of being crazy for six months. You needn't look suspicious of me now. I'm all right, like various other political aspirants. But for six months I was as crazy as a bed bug, and dangerous, too. I'm rather proud of the latter fact, for I would hate to think that I was an imbecile. It all came from a head-slugging that I received at the hands of thugs. Three of them attacked me one night, and after pounding me senseless took my money and adjourned 'sine die.' Then I went crazy. I remember just a little of my insane career. I know that I had a horror of something always and that something was forever changing, as it was undefinable. I wanted to get away, out anywhere, just so I should be going. And they wouldn't let me. Who? Why giants, devils, dragons, elfs, unknown animals with great misshapen heads and mean, distorted faces. They were forever with me, one at a time. At times I was afraid and sat in one corner watching the creature in the other corner that was forever watching me and telling me that I could not escape, and then I thought I was alone for a moment. The fiendish guard was gone. I would break out and run away. Then the door was barred and I would break it down. I tried, though. I tried to tear the bars apart, to twist and bend them, to gnaw them in two, but without success. While I was doing this my devil guard would come back and stand outside the bars and laugh at me. Then I would be punished by it, and, oh! how I endeavored to kill it in those struggles—but I invariably failed. Finally the number of my guards grew less and did not look so fierce. They went away more often and remained away longer. Then I thought there was only one, and even that one became indistinct, and I was only troubled by a constant fear of its return. But the fear grew less and less, until finally it passed away, and I regained my good horse sense."

[*6 March 1893, p. 5, no. 6*]

No. 124.

T he true bent of the primitive mind of man relative to his social state was forcibly and humorously illustrated to me this morning," began Fahrney Teller, who is at the Southern. "It was over in one of the large office buildings where a porter was polishing window plate and brass etchings. He seemed much dissatisfied with his work and murmured along, accompanying his words with movements which contained more of grace than energy. 'Men work,' he soliloquized. 'Ketch me doin' this ef I didn' jes' haf to. If I didn' have no wife I wouldn' be here now, I tell ye. Allus comin' aroun' wantin' summin' to eat. 'Specs I goin' to feed her.' Then his great heart was burdened to breaking with the thought of the obligatory mandates of matrimony, and he broke out with: 'Better she treat me kind, mighty kind, I'm thinkin'. She better never set her heart on diamonds. Fine diamonds she'll get out o' me shinin' windows. Yes, better treat me mighty kind ur I won't work,' and

with that he gathered up his pail and departed. The conditions of modern civilization are too much for this conception. In Africa or Asia he would rapidly reverse these foolish American ideas, and it is safe to say that he would be moderately happy if his wife supported herself and him and treated him kindly. She would have to practice economy withal, or he might not make ends meet."

[*7 March 1893, p. 7, no. 5*]

No. 125.

V egetarianism is a delusion and snare," said Henry C. Maddox, who is at the Lindell. "Look at the Chinese, the Japanese and India's millions, who subsist chiefly on vegetable foods, are smaller in stature, shorter lived and mentally and physically weaker than the people of the English or German nation, who use a flesh dietary. All starch foods are a strain upon the digestive powers. The nitrogen they supply to the system is not ample recompense for the trouble they cause. A proof of this is found in the phenomenal benefits accruing to invalids by the use of the Salisbury diet, which consists exclusively of the lean of beef or mutton and water. At the German spas the physicians insist upon a greatly diminished quantity of bread, no potatoes and plenty of meat, eggs and milk. Milk, eggs, cheese, fish, flesh and fowl, the world over, furnish an ample supply of nitrogen in a form more easily digested than vegetables."

[*14 March 1893, p. 7, no. 3*]

No. 126.

"The Chinese think our way of making tea barbarous," said Theodore Halevy at the Southern. "They make and drink their tea differently from us. We draw our tea and let it stand. In China they pour boiling water into a cup and turn some tea into it, and when the leaves sink to the bottom, which happens in a few seconds, they pour the water off and drink it. The result of our way is that the tannin is squeezed out of the stewed tea leaves and we get a strong and bitter decoction which helps to wreck our nerves instead of the gentle stimulant that the Chinese beverage amounts to."

[*20 March 1893, p. 5, no. 2*]

No. 127.

"Why does Russia linger in ignorance," answered David S. Jordan to a friend in the Southern. "Let me tell you a story. When I was in college at Cornell there came a bright young Russian to study by the name of Dabrolohoff. This young man was of quick perceptive powers and deeply interested in the progressive practical sciences and questions. He studied very hard for four years, did much more work than any single term required, and graduated with the honors of his class. He removed to New York and entered into a successful practice of civil engineering. Some time later I learned that he had gone back to his native land. I heard no more of this young man outside of a few scientific articles in some European magazines for nearly ten years. While making a tour of Europe and Russia I bethought myself of him and wondered why his brilliant parts had not long since brought him into prominence. In Russia I made inquiries and there learned, to my astonishment and sorrow, that the student had been suspected of treason, tried and sentenced to Siberia, where he had died in filth and chains. Do you imagine that a country which hides the light of its young genius beneath the bushel of despotism can grow intellectually?"

[*20 March 1893, p. 5, no. 4*]

No. 128.

"The ingenious disposition of some people would augur that they would some day attain name and fame from their work," said Harry Valentine, who is at the Lindell. "They have wonderful

95

ability in the line of making knick-knacks and devices that do queer work, but somehow they never bring about anything useful. They spend their existence idly going through life with a jack-knife and a pine stick looking for a shady resting-place whereat to sit down and whittle a nothing. Every hamlet in the land has one of these, every village two, every county seat three, and every city several hundred. Some explain the uselessness of this class by saying that they have never had any education; that they are of a philosophical turn of mind, and that proper mental training would have made them wonderful men. I won't post any opinion on this matter whatever, but I will recall the work of a Savannah (Ga.) man who recently exhibited an American flag made of acorns entirely. He took the trouble to string all those acorns, thousands of them, on cat-gut strings, and then to tint the cups and shells with the tri-color in a most beautiful manner. He mounted the flag on a fine varnished pole and hung it on his wall to dry. As the acorns dry out the flag will become exceedingly light, while its beauty will be enhanced. Still the utter uselessness of the flag makes it ridiculous."

[*22 March 1893, p. 7, no. 2*]

No. 129.

"A phenomenon which I had occasion to observe some years ago, relative to fast time," said Harrison Wild, who is at the Lindell, "was the rapid traveling of an earthquake shock. To the mind a thing so destructive and disastrous would always be conceived as traveling slowly, rolling along with irresistible force, but only slowly. One would imagine that the power that makes the great earth's crust tremble would be compelled to stay a moment in order to accomplish the work. I was relieved of this idea some fifteen years ago, when as a telegraph operator I manipulated the key in the city of San Francisco. I was in charge of one end of the Pacific Cable Company's ocean wire, and many a night I talked and joked with the American operator who held the other end at Tokio. I remember one decidedly sultry night, I was almost ready to fall asleep in my office chair, a signal came from Tokio. The operator there stated that an earthquake shock had just been felt—a very severe shock—which did much damage. He said that it came from the northwest and was traveling southeast across the Pacific towards California. He closed with the irritating words, 'Look out.' I laughed to myself at the foolish remark, because I believed the shock would spend its force long before it reached California, and at any rate it would not arrive for days. Just twelve hours later a distinct tremor struck San Francisco, and was immediately recorded as an earthquake. Now, then, Tokio is 4500 miles from San Francisco and the earthquake came in twelve hours, or at the rate of six miles a minute — 360 miles an hour. How is that for time?"

[*22 March 1893, p. 7, no. 3*]

No. 130.

We have nowadays the Pessimists and the Optimists," said James L. Notall, who is at the Laclede. "The first maintaining that the world is worse than it ever was before, and the second arguing that it is better than it ever was before. There is room for wide and inexplicable argument here which is daily utilized by both sides. I will offer as my mite the following tale, which will no doubt cause further argument: The old nations which inhabited Asia Minor — Byzantium — were, as historians well know, decidedly cultured, possessing excellent devices of many kinds, great temples and dwellings which were possessed of many comforts that we know of and many more that have passed probably into oblivion. A fruit of their intellectual development was the fact that they possessed a medium of exchange, namely of gold and silver in the shape of coin of the realm. These coins were marked with the sovereign's seal and often times his profile. Furthermore all specimens so far secured of the money in question is either of pure

silver or gold without alloy of any kind, which shows that the nations in question were desirous of a sound currency much after the fashion of the level-headed Americans of to-day. But recently, among the ruins of a now forgotten city, an urn of excellent pottery of that ancient time was unearthed, and upon examination it was found to contain a number of coins of that time — rudely carved, indeed, but equal to the best specimens in existence. These pieces were found, upon further examination, however, to be of base metal, though fashioned in imitation of the genuine. Now the question naturally arises, were there counterfeiters away back in the dim past? If so, when did evil begin, and is the world really getting worse or better?"

[*22 March 1893, p. 7, no. 4*]

No. 131.

About the most ludicrous thing that I ever ran across in my life," said Edgar Tallman, who is at the Lindell, "was a convention of poets and literary writers, which convened in the town of Warsaw, Ind., some three years ago. They were the poets and literary writers of the Northwestern States, including Illinois, Indiana, Ohio, Michigan, and Wisconsin. The purpose of the convention was mutual improvement and the betterment of the poetic vein in men. Just think of it, a convention of poets. Well sir,

97

I've seen many samples of the spring poet, the summer poet, the fall and winter poet, but I never did see such an aggregation of long-haired, distracted looking individuals in all my life. They were interesting. I met them strolling through Spring Fountain Park, of that town, just after one of the morning sessions had adjourned. They gathered in groups and discussed the merits of Shakespeare, Browning, etc. By a very foolish move on my part I gave one an opportunity to produce a poetic scroll, which he let unwind to the ground and then began reading from it in an ecstatic manner that made me long for mother and home. Joking aside, the idea of such a convention borders upon the insane. Such a meeting of men of genius would be most unsatisfactory. True genius is a true and polished sphere, around which the world may gather to admire. But the other spheres can not gather round. They can but meet and touch at some small point and no more. Genius brooks no competitor—acknowledges no peer—and so in my estimation the most positive proof that one might have relative as to whether these Indiana poets had any ability whatever was the simple fact that they met in convention. It proves that they did not have any at all."

[*22 March 1893, p. 7, no. 5*]

No. 132.

I hear a group of gentlemen over there discussing art and the money that can be made out of the artistic faculty," said Edgar Wales, who is at the Southern. "Whenever I hear a discussion of that kind it makes me think that we haven't any art at all to-day. We haven't any great genius of any kind that I know of. Where is there now a great living poet, a great painter, a great sculptor, a masterful writer? We simply bow low and say there are none—not one. This is the futilitarian age—the age for inventors and of them, for men who can think out some device for lightening the labor of man and making money real fast—a thoroughly commonplace, unartistic and practical age. Those gentlemen there when they bring in a mercenary consideration destroy all the thought of real artistic work. Not long ago I came across a worker in ivory, an engraver. This man was poor—was artless in appearance, and earned a scanty living by repairing and engraving monograms on small knickknacks. Being a kind of crank on the score of the true artistic spirit I was indefinably drawn to this man and his work, so that I became a frequent visitor at his den. When I knew him better he condescended to show me an ivory carving of an ordinary workman with a paper cap on and a hammer in his hand. I looked at the little gem, for it was a gem, and began to ponder over its beauty. 'How long have you worked on this?' I asked. 'Three years,' he said, 'but it is not yet finished.' 'When it is done,' said I, 'what can you get for it?' 'I do not know and I do not care,' was the reply. 'When it is done what will you do with it?' 'Put it away and make another.' Now, then, there was the true genius. The lover of beauty for beauty's sake—not for the fame it would bring nor the money. It is such a temperament as this that gives to the world its beauty and its life."

[*22 March 1893, p. 7, no. 6*]

No. 133.

A s a compiler of statistics and a student of social conditions I have recently made some studies that may be interesting," said F. T. Croyden, who is at the Lindell. "It is in reference to the effect that the time or easy payment credit system has upon the people throughout the land. I have studied this phase of the social problem in three of the largest cities in the country, and find the system to be an evil influence at work among the poor classes. To do this I have been compelled to be a collector, and visit daily a certain number of persons where payments fell due weekly or monthly. The goods on which the payments were made were of decidedly small value—articles being sold for $5 and $10 and being paid 25¢ a week or $1 a month. Now all these goods were sold in the small homes where the parties could not pay cash, but had a craving for fine furnishings which

they satisfied with a cheap semblance of luxury. This was one of the evil results. A second was that this little payment system taught them to shirk their duty of promptly paying it. It taught them to put off the bill week after week until the whole was due and then to avoid payment by all sorts of excuses and subterfuges, the practice of which is degrading. A continued period of this kind of buying makes of these people what the dealers term bad cases. They are no good—have learned to steal in this round-about manner, which becomes apparent even to the children of the home, and inculcates evil in them."

[*27 March 1893, p. 5, no. 1*]

No. 134.

I wonder how it comes about," said J. T. Abrams, who is at the Southern, "that a beautiful face of which you only had one glance at in all your life can live so vividly in your memory. Mine was a mere passing glance. Why, confound it all, every time a chilly rain drizzles down all day long and makes everything lonesome and cold, then I feel like getting off alone and looking out on the dull earth—just to think of that one face. It has been so long now, nearly twelve years since I met a pale-faced girl in New York coming along Fifty-first street. It was just such a day as this, with muddy streets and drizzling rain to beat everything. Some dark brown curls were loosened by the wind and lay limp and wet against her forehead. I observed all this in passing by and I imagined that the girl was hungry or homeless, or both, but I couldn't tell; all I could do was simply to turn and look after. I have traveled nearly around the world since then in Asia, Africa and Europe and out through the lonesome, dreary mining camps of the West, but I haven't been able to forget that face. On bright days I wonder little about her, but every time it rains I feel this way. I know away down near the Cape of Good Hope I sat one entire morning looking out and seeing that girl's face in the wet leaves of the trees and pools of water held in basins of mud. It was always one thought: What did that girl want? — whether she was hungry and cold, or homeless and cold, or both, and why didn't I help her? Queer, isn't it?"

[*27 March 1893, p. 5, no. 2*]

No. 135.

The power of the mind to delude itself is simply marvelous," said Darious Manes, who is at the Laclede. "How people conceive themselves that certain actions of theirs or state of thought move the infinite to definite action is simply marvelous. Not over a year ago a friend of mine was seized with a dangerous illness which threatened his life and worse. He immediately was seized with remorse for past offenses in the face of coming dissolution and sought by prayers and offerings to satisfy the wrath of the Great Unknown. He became so overwrought with worry that he was moved to tears, and on more than one occasion did various things which afterwards in good health he admitted were ludicrous and idiotic. No change for the better came for a long time until a change of physicians was effected. Then he began to regain health and the sickness was eventually cured. That was not the best nor worst of it all. During his return journey to health he attributed all his buoyant feelings and recovery to the devotions of himself and others offered to the Maker, and stated that the Lord must have guided the second physician to him or him to the second physician — it didn't matter much which, just so the Lord did it. I talked with his physician afterward, and we began discussing the cure and finally drifted in the fellow's religious revolution as related to his cure. The physician figured out that he would have been cured a month sooner if he had rested his mind and quit asking the Lord for anything at all — or begging for Divine intercession. I believe my friend agrees with that opinion now — but you see just how far a well-balanced mind can really delude itself."

[*27 March 1893, p. 5, no. 4*]

No. 136.

A friend of mine has just sent me this stone hatchet," said Clark J. Nelson, who is at the Lindell, "undoubtedly from one of the mounds about here. Such a gift as this invariably carries me back to that dim period of which we know absolutely nothing about except that these mounds remain containing all these relics that indicate a rude civilization. Such a relic coming to me is much like a meteor from out the clouds, that would speak of other spheres, if I could not see them so plainly. Just up and around this one little implement of stone a man can build all the details of a civilization with rude camps and log fires, with all the dark forest about, burning like a divine watchlight set over the cradle of intelligence and freedom. Or you can change the thought and make it of a vast tribe, wild in the extreme, with some rough thought of fellowship urging them to unite against the common enemy — to band together and so protect themselves against the cold, hunger, wild beasts and all the untoward conditions that beset the life of primeval man. It's rather inspiring to me, and yet it is only a stone implement which is very commonplace and of absolutely no value whatever. It sets one to thinking by what possibility could the present grand civilization wane and become extinct."

[*28 March 1893, p. 7, no. 4*]

No. 137.

What is there about a book agent or a peddler of any kind that is so distasteful to the ordinary citizen of to-day?" said Martin Cole, who is at the Laclede. "The efforts of these people to make a living is conscientious, and I am positive there is no work on the face of the earth that is half so wearisome or soul-trying as this one thing of canvassing books. There is no satisfaction in it, and not even a good living. Everyone turns with disgust from the book agent. Probably it is because people can not brook anything outside of the regular lines of trade. They prefer to have things in their proper places — books in a book store, candy in a candy store and the like throughout the long list of earthly articles that we use. Then they want the stores close at hand, so that they can rush out and secure what they want, paying spot cash for it. These are what people term the legitimate lines of trade and they are. Then when a peddler arrives the merchant or the ordinary citizen immediately figures out that anything that must be brought about to him to effect a sale must not be good; it is outside the legitimate line, and if it was good it would simply be placed upon the market through the ordinary channels and left for the public to conceive its merits. So then I figure out that this dissatisfaction with book-agents and the like resolves itself into the great law of order, which is an innate desire in the heart of everyone."

[*28 March 1893, p. 7, no. 5*]

No. 138.

It has been noted by all zoologists and sociologists that animals are governed by instinct," said Russell J. Langman, who is at the Southern. "Just how to define instinct has not yet been explained, but it is some governing law by which all brutes are guided and which they never break. It would almost seem that many consider it impossible for animals to do anything that could possibly hurt themselves. This instinct is supposed to tell them when they have enough to eat and drink, when what they eat is wholesome and when not, guides them away from all poisonous plants and keeps them from any dangerous overexertion such as we humans plunge into and knowingly continue until we are worn out and ready to die. I am inclined to doubt this theory, for I have tried various experiments with animals and have found their instinct at times very poor. For instance I gave a young rat a cage with a treadwheel attachment. The treadwheel proved so very enjoyable that the rat simply ran itself to death, which shows that brutes can not judge or limit their pleasure. Cats love catnip, as it is called. Delight to roll in it and eat it. I mixed a moderate amount of nightshade with the catnip plant and of-

fered it to my home domestic. The cat ate of it, never distinguishing between the poison and the catnip and consequently died. I fail to observe where the governing instinct came in at, in these two instances at least."

[*28 March 1893, p. 7, no. 6*]

No. 139.

It is now asserted by many that a man can — or a woman, either — be overeducated," said T. E. Harper, who is at the Southern. "People meet so many cads and cranks who are 'educated' that they have really begun to assert that a person may be overeducated — know too much. Good old American horse sense will outgrow this idea soon, I know. It isn't education that is troubling the cads and long-haired cranks. It isn't knowing too much that is troubling any one. It's the simple fact that a minor knowledge of a hundred arts and sciences has succeeded in bewildering these people. They run to this meeting and that 4 o'clock Spencer class, and this 2 o'clock class for the study of Ibsen, and that evening class for the instantaneous acquirement of a supreme knowledge of the German master works until they have become befuddled. They don't actually know what they are doing, and so they gather about and talk on a dozen subjects, only to make some poor striving soul imagine that he doesn't know anything at all and that they are supreme. As a matter of fact, they are wasting their time, and so is any one else who listens to them. This class it is that fills our public school courses with drawing, music, foreign languages, painting and a crew of other foolish studies. It isn't overeducation. The man who studies constantly on one subject — tries to be perfect in that — he is never over-educated, and never will be. When will our long-headed, common-sense Americans awake and see this?"

[*28 March 1893, p. 7, no. 7*]

No. 140.

T he most remarkable thing that has ever occurred to me in my earthly career," said Eugene McKelsey, who is at the Southern, "occurred some years ago when I was still afflicted with dyspepsia. I had a bad case, I assure you. Oh, I was all broke up. Food was disgusting. I had no appetite, and I just walked around looking for some place to lay down and die. Some time passed and I grew worse. I saw myself a physical wreck, and try as I might I simply couldn't revive appetite nor ambition. Finally I ran into an old woman, a kind of witch, I guess — old women are always witches when they dress in faded garments and predict to you — who said that I would get well if I should go to a certain farm and three times a day cast an ear of corn to a white pig and then listen to it eat. I do not believe

in such rites, but, dear me, I was so sick that I was willing to try anything. So I bought a white pig, secured a pen for it within the mentioned farm limits, and daily made three journeys with an ear of corn that I threw in and then watched the pig eat. Well, do you know the sound of that pig crunching and sucking those corn grains made me hungry. Oh, I enjoyed the sensation so much. It made me ravenous. When I returned from my walk I wanted to eat. So I continued visiting the white pig and eating three good meals a day until I was myself again and as healthy as I am now. I don't care to understand the whyness of it now. I am only too glad to be well."

[*29 March 1893, p. 7, no. 3*]

No. 141.

I would like to be a good, artistic, voluble, whole-souled liar," said Peter Linn, who is at the Lindell. "Really, I would. I don't object to a good liar at all, providing he lies consistently. The only reason that I don't lie myself is simply because I forget too easy, and so I would be sure to make a break and then I would be compelled to bear the mortification of having to explain. At the period that I thought to become a liar I was deterred by an example which I will always remember. There used to be an old cuss in our town who came into our store, where I was clerking, to loaf. He would climb up on a little stool, big as he was, and nicely poise himself on his lower spinal extremity, and then rock to and fro in that position. He always had good long stories — wild bear stories — suitable for Nimrods. One day he told how he went hunting one balmy, sunshiny, soft spring morning — how he hunted all day. He lingered over each little detail and described minutely the color of his game, the number of prongs on the great buck's antlers that he shot as a climax to his day's hunt. He told his story so artistically, so minutely, and used such excellent language, that it seemed all to be good and true. I was entranced. I didn't care whether it was a lie or not, because it was artistic; but he wound up his story by saying that the only reason he did not bring home all that game was simply because the load would have made him break through the heavy snow crust — and he could not walk that way."

[*29 March 1893, p. 7, no. 4*]

No. 142.

The massiveness of ancient architecture is constantly exploited by that class of modern students who make a study of the old and constantly live in the past," said E. Gray Smith, who is at the Lindell. "Every ancient bit of architecture, painting, sculpture and carving is looked upon by these worshipers of the old as superior to

anything achieved since or to be yet achieved. Many thriving geniuses have brought these foolish students and critics to their senses at times, but only by some artifice that placed the latter in such a ridiculous position that their attacks upon the new became more venomous than ever. They rake up the old aqueducts at Rome and tell with awe that the Anio aqueduct was sixty-three miles long. Why don't they tell us about the iron-pipe conduit that leads across three States from East Ohio to Chicago and carries crude oil from the rich fields to the manufacturing center. They relate the ponderous height of the pillars of a temple at Karnak in Egypt, but no one of them gives any credit to the modern sky-scraper that often stands a skeleton of steel, twenty stories high, before a brick or stone is laid of the environing wall. Such buildings have been put up in eleven months in this country, like the Masonic Temple in Chicago and the Union Trust building in this city. The Romans built their sixty-three mile aqueduct in about 100 years, and the Temple of Karnak was building still longer. We haven't lost anything by the lapse of years — not a continental thing."

[*29 March 1893, p. 7, no. 5*]

No. 143.

This thing of hypnotism is certainly a mysterious force," said John J. King, who is at the Southern. "It isn't a question of whether a man is educated or possesses any superior mentality in exercising or gaining control over this force; it is simply the question, is he physically constructed with this element of force in him? Hypnotists and mesmerists are by a large majority ignorant. They do not make any remarkable use of their power. Usually, it is left to the onlooker, the casual investigator, to make the strong tests. I think I can explain this power up to the point of a subtle force, like electricity and magnetism, but there I must stop, as even electricians must stop. Here, for instance, is Tesla, the electrician, who can create that mystic force, electricity, draw it to him and through him until it illuminates an incandescent bulb in one of his lifted hands. He is physically a dynamo—a force creator, drawing from the beyond the elements of force that in him become a current and a light. Here, also, are the hypnotists, able to physically collect the elements of hypnotic force and change it to a current that passes from them into their subject and makes his comprehension theirs. This hypnotic force is magnetic, for a hypnotist can draw the active form of his subject after him, or his cold, stiff, entranced figure, either, for that matter. It does not matter. Electricity is magnetic also. This current (hypnotic) rushes into the subject and gives him infinite strength, at the same time making him impervious to pain, able to withstand any weight or strain. Tesla's late performances have cleared much relative to this awe-inspiring hypnotic force."

[*29 March 1893, p. 7, no. 6*]

No. 144.

Isn't it pretty near time something was being done toward educating the criminal classes?" said A. T. Born, who is at the Lindell. "I've seen so much of criminal correction and so little of actual good resulting from it that I actually wonder how people can live along and not endeavor to strengthen the minds of the criminals by proper example and enforced study than by trying to weaken and break down their bodies so as to incapacitate them for further wrong-doing. I say this because I think the present Penitentiary and convict lease system is nothing more than a breaking-down system. I have even heard criminals who had long been schooled in vice and crime complain, and for once in truthful earnest, that they never had a chance to learn anything. I have also heard younger men of the same class— mere boys on the road to ruin—ask for permission to learn something. Not over a few days ago a young fellow came before a criminal court Judge to be sentenced for burglary. He exclaimed after the sentence, 'Can't yer make it House of Correc-

105

tion, yer Honer? I'd like to go some place where I can learn something.' There is no getting around the issue. Sensible people can not ignore the fact that something must be done for the criminals in the way of education or they will always remain criminals."

[*30 March 1893, p. 7, no. 2*]

No. 145.

This week is Holy Week, isn't it?" said O. L. Krieger, who is at the Southern. "That brings up the question of ill-luck, because Holy Week brings Black Friday, and that is supposed to be an especially unlucky day. I never lost anything on a Friday, nor I don't remember of starting any enterprise on Friday, so I can't tell whether such enterprises turn out unlucky or not. But Black Friday is here, and it brings up the whole train of incidents that I have heard related by friends of how they did certain things on a Friday, and how they lost or got hurt, or did something else equally as bad. Capt. Anson started East on Friday with thirteen men in his baseball club, and lost every game until he got home again, when the ill-luck was somewhat reversed. I have a friend who is extremely unlucky, and is afraid to enter into any kind of a deal, because of losing. He says he was born on Friday and now he is sorry for it. Now he thinks that nothing but whisky will aid him to

stave off his trouble, and so he never gets sober any more. But I know of one instance where Friday was lucky. 'Monte Carlo' Wells, the man who very nearly broke the Monaco bank, made his first great winning of $50,000 on a Friday, and it makes me doubt the old superstition. Winning $50,000 on Friday would break any man's prejudice."

[*30 March 1893, p. 7, no. 3*]

No. 146.

The Amazon warriors supposed to have existed prehistorically, and at present in Dahomey, have long been the cause and source of much humor and investigation upon the part of that class of mankind who ever rejoice to see a woman do something bold," said W. I. Goldsmith, who is at the Laclede. "Historians, sedate and serious old writers, both in and out of the Church; monks in grewsome cowls and lonely convents, satirical old celibates and rampant writers of profane history, all without exception linger a little longer on the subject of Amazon warriors than they do on any other one subject of equal importance. One would almost have enjoyed being alongside of one of them while he was writing on the subject, and to have clinched him between the ribs and said, 'Eh, old sport.' It's safe to say that a monk or celibate could not help but laugh over it. Most of them would have enjoyed being king with Amazon warriors. But modern evils are playing havoc with the theme. Amazon warriors figure often and profusely in all sorts of literature. Any great daily will buy dispatches of any length relative to movements among Amazons down in that two-cent country of Dahomey. The latest joke is that the Amazon warriors have applied or petitioned their king in Dahomey for decollete armor. If the Dahomeyan King knew how much free advertising he is getting he would star in a theatrical company."

[*30 March 1893, p. 7, no. 4*]

No. 147.

I was once compelled to witness a fearful wreck on the Erie and Western road near Salem, N.Y.," said William St. John, who is at the Lindell. "It is all bad enough to be accidentally a momentary witness to a great calamity — to be aware of it for ever so short a time — but to know that unsuspecting souls are being whirled to certain death and not to be able to do something is simply awful. One afternoon in November of 1889 I was strolling some ten miles from Salem along the railroad track and came upon a burning bridge culvert that had, no doubt, been set on fire by a spark from some passing train. It was in an exceedingly barren district just where a rocky ravine led across the road's path, deep and narrow, with a small stream winding its way out of the hills. I could do nothing except start for the nearest house to get men who would take up guard positions at equal distances from the culvert and signal approaching trains. I had barely figured this out and started to accomplish it when I heard the distant rumbling of a train that was rapidly approaching. I started to run down the track to head it off by signals, but too late. It approached so rapidly that before I was 100 yards away it was on me. The engineer heeded the signal and did all he could to stop — then jumped. A fearful wreck followed, in which fourteen were killed and many injured — and I was compelled to see it all. The nervous shock and strain of excitement that followed laid me up for fully a week afterwards."

[*30 March 1893, p. 7, no. 6*]

No. 148.

I never understood the art of fishing and I never expect to," said C. Porter Coleman, who is at the Lindell. "I have gone fishing time and again. Some of the longest and best hours of my life have been spent in endeavoring to delude a measly squad of fish to hang around my hook and let me catch them, but I now count those hours wasted. Fishing to me is a vast and hollow sham. If a fat and shining minnow isn't tempting enough, or a well-fed, not to say almost pampered, fishworm is not bait sufficient, then I beg leave to stick my pole in the mud and quit even. Why, I've seen the time that I've plugged around an entire afternoon and on into the shadows of night, with a coal-scoop and a growler, upturning whole sidewalks, for which afterwards I had to pay the city, laying waste an entire spring garden that I might present the pick and choice of wormhood to a few elite residents of fishdom, only to have them ogled at from a respectful distance without even having my cork disturbed—no, siree—not even my cork. I have risen before the sun, tramped seven miles and rowed about all day to keep within close proximity of people who were simply pulling out fish by the score, only to see my pick and choice coldly snubbed by the same fish that would pass 20 feet farther on and swallow a measly bedbug or grubworm on some one else's hook just to show me that I wasn't in it. Bedbug, I say, hook and all. Don't you say go fishing to me. I won't hear of it. I'm done with fishing now and forever. Amen."

[*3 April 1893, p. 5, no. 4*]

No. 149.

Every time it rains like it does to-night," said Malcolm Withers, who was at the Lindell Monday night, "I get a peculiar feeling of wanting to be alone. If I can just be alone in my room with several windows to look out from I feel excellent, and decidedly reminiscent. I delight to hear the rain pelt against my windows and catch a glimpse of sheets of wind-driven rain in the glare of an electric flash. A night like this I am in the best of humor with myself, although I prove very unsatisfactory company to any one else, for I do not care to talk at all. The best part of it all is to listen to the long shrill whistle of trains that are far out on the road, either entering or leaving the city. Just to hear the sound die away on the night as it comes, driven through the night and the rain by such a furious wind is delightful. I learned to care for this sound when I was still a boy, keeping regular hours and being sent to bed just a little after 10 o'clock. At that time a regular freight train passed through our town at 10:15, and only stopped for water. I always enjoyed listening from my cot in a drowsy manner to the rumbling of the cars pulling in and stopping. I enjoyed hearing the start, the whistle once for brakes and the steaming away. The sound of the cars rattling and bumping, but growing fainter and fainter as the speed increased, was always music to me, and when the sound had all but died out of hearing as the train hurried northward the sound of the long, sharp whistle came back, modified by distance, however, until it was all music. It just seemed to open the gates of dreamland, for I invariably fell asleep."

[*12 April 1893, p. 7, no. 3*]

No. 150.

"The clearest judgment often circumvents itself by a disregard of the very little things," said J. Templeton Fay, who is at the Southern. "What I mean is that a judgment may be ever so clear and yet not be able to judge its own interests successfully. I saw this illustrated somewhat over a year ago, while I was in St. Petersburg, Russia. Every one is familiar with the condition of the Russian people, and with the methods of the police to circumscribe the nihilistic movement at all times. One of the brightest leaders of this secret band at that time was Ivan Estrogoff, a young Russian, the son of well to do parents, who lived in Moscow. Estrogoff had been educated abroad, had studied civil engineering and mechanical science, until he was well fitted to be successful even in the service of his own country. Somehow the downtrodden Russians interested him more. He found more congenial company among the nihilists, the individuals of which were, many of them, highly educated, and of the upper circle, but dissatisfied. Estrogoff, as developed later, quickly distinguished himself among them as a leader, for he prepared a code of signals anew each month, so that the police might not discover them, and prepared adroit circulars for the scattered members in a manner that was remarkable. The circulars apparently indicated nothing. One of these circulars accidentally fell into the hands of the police. It meant nothing to them, of course, but Russian police are so ignorant that they are suspicious of everything, and consequently the circular was retained and worked upon as a clew. His laundryman, an agent of the secret police, found in his room a bundle of the circulars, which he removed and deposited with the Prefect. In this Estrogoff's clear judgment was circumvented, for the very meaninglessness of the bills made them dangerous and full of meaning. He was shadowed as only the Russian police can shadow a man. His laundryman, his servants, his attendants, one and all, became the agents of police until it was discovered that he was preparing monthly circulars of similar nature. Evidence was trumped up against him; he was seized and tried, receiving as his sentence a term in Siberia."

[*12 April 1893, p. 7, no. 5*]

No. 151.

"The northern half of the Island of Borneo is the queerest and most unsatisfactory place to live that one can imagine," said Burton Emhoff, who is at the Laclede. "It is a land of constant recurring phenomena, where cyclones are frequent and deluges of water very common. The vegetation in that half is very fine, but in all probability the wildest and most tangled on earth—not even excepting that of Africa. The cause of all the trouble is the shallow condition of the sea north of it, great shoals of sand existing a few miles out which extend along its entire northern length. These shoals are covered by a depth of water not over 5 feet deep. The constant recurring winds that blow in that climate change to hurricanes and sweep the smaller islands of all visible life. When such a storm strikes the sand shoals north of Borneo it sweeps up the shallow salt water into its course and drenches the island with it. Often it gathers up sand, great masses of it, from the clear swept shoal and whirls it for miles high over the island, carrying it into the inland and scattering it everywhere. The work of these storms does not always end with that. Entire shoals of fish, of all sizes, have been swept up time and again by the fierce winds with the water and sand and scattered about Borneo. In some places the ground would be literally covered with fish, enough to supply a heavy population for weeks. But such luck is no reparation for the evil the winds do and consequently the northern half will never be inhabited by those who value their lives."

[*19 April 1893, p. 7, no. 4*]

No. 152.

I do believe there is a great deal more of the ridiculous in this world than there is of the sublime," said Philip Durham, who is stopping at the Lindell. "Human nature occasionally struggles up to the pinnacle of fame. Some persons are energetic, patient, stern and possessed of broad mental balance enough, so that they eventually become sublime and alone of their kind, but that is not often. If they do so, you usually observe them broken physically, dissatisfied, remembering little of any worldly pleasure and much of worldly pain. That has been the record of almost every master mind that has come 'out of sterility into eternity again,' as Carlyle would say. The ridiculous is more apparent, for every-day people have only to do with every-day annoyances. One of the most ridiculous things that this life presents can be observed in my birthplace, Whitney, Vt. It is that of two old residents, both of them now in their 70th year, cordially despising one another for no reason at all. All Whitney is aware of the enmity that old Jerry Evans bears to old Billy Sykes, and it is made the subject of much waggish by-play. Old Uncle Jerry and old Uncle Billy are both natives of Whitney. They were raised in proximity to each other, attended the same school, knew the same village girls and conducted their local interests as men side by side for years. There was no particular issue between them except a cordial dislike, and they constantly opposed one another. This opposition brought up one additional wrong after another until each had a long list of grievances to relate. They have never settled with each other and never will, simply taking it all out in bad language and glaring pomposity of demeanor when they are near one another. That is what I call the ridiculous side of life when human beings act so queer. What a contrast, I have often thought, they present to those truly grand natures that are born into the world, living alone, poor, but always at peace, giving their life and strength to the thoughts of a better way for human beings to live and leaving that as a legacy."

[*19 April 1893, p. 7, no. 6*]

No. 153.

W hen some one says hoodoo and refers to ill-luck's following the curse or wish of some one's that evil may fall upon some one else, I invariably feel like saying superstitious," said Gilbert Woodward, who is at Hurst's. "Hoodooing people is something I do not believe in at all, because I have never been hoodooed myself. There was a colored man who died not long since in Rock Island, Ill., while I was there, who claimed to be hoodooed. His case was certainly remarkable. This negro was shot in the back and also in the left knee by some one whom he claimed he had never seen. The way he explained it was that he long before secured the enmity of a negro woman there who was a fortune-teller and necromancer by profession. The woman threatened him with punishment if he did not return a certain charm that he had taken from

her, which consisted of seven hairs of various colors from seven different animals. Upon his failure to return it within a specified time he was shot by some one whom he did not see, and seriously wounded. The fortune-teller also visited him and threw a wine glass at him, which he did not hear fall to the floor. He insisted constantly that his leg would never get well and that the fortune-teller was piercing his right arm with needles. As a matter of fact, his leg grew constantly worse, although the wound at first was small, and was finally amputated. The right arm became poisoned of something, and after a short siege of inflammation the negro died, protesting up to the last moment of his life that the fortune-teller — Big Annie — had hoodooed him out of the world. The attending physicians, while protesting that the negro must be demented, could not explain the constant decline in the man's health. Big Annie was also found, and would say nothing, except that the victim ought to die."

[*20 April 1893, p. 7, no. 4*]

No. 154.

I joined in with an Englishman last summer on the queerest voyage imaginable," said Rowan M. Hunter, who is at the Laclede. "He was on his way to the east coast of the Red Sea to look for a leather gripsack which he supposed contained a great deal of money. The grip had been the property of his brother, a gold-seeker in Australia, who had been decidedly successful. The ship that brought him back sank in the Red Sea near the Asiatic shore, giving the crew just sufficient time to escape with their lives. The grip and money went down. The fury of the storm wrecked the ship past all recovery, and no attempt was made to recover any of its freightage. The brother from Australia took sick in Asia Minor, but made his way to Constantinople, where he died in an American hospital. He wrote a letter to his brother in England, and related to him the misfortunes that had befallen him and the value of the gripsack that had gone down. My acquaintance, the living brother, was going by way of boat to the nearest point of the wreck and there proposed to formulate and complete all necessary arrangements for the search and recovery of the valuable grip. He had brought along with him an expert diver and diving apparatus sufficient for the needs of the search. I left him at Alexandria for a run through Egypt and wished him success, because he was a jolly good fellow. About six months afterward I met him in Paris, where he was spending a few weeks. There he told that he had recovered the grip a good distance from the supposed spot, and that it contained enough of wealth to keep him excellently through life. That was a more than remarkable case of luck, I thought."

[*21 April 1893, p. 7, no. 4*]

No. 155.

"There is no more interesting sight in all Europe than the catacombs of Rome," began Benner Heckard who is at the Southern. "One can see the ordinary routine sights of them any day for a small sum of money, and they are well worth visiting. I fancy, however, that I saw something a great long way from the ordinary while on my visit there. Last August I was in Rome and paid a visit to the catacombs alone. I did not care for company, as such sights always appeal more effectively to me when there is no one along to comment on them. I secured a guide and we started on the long journey. We passed the vaults of the celebrated saints, on the shelf-life receptacles where a narrow box was all that could be given to the sainted dead. I saw the narrow chambers of prayer where altar and walls were decorated with the bones and skulls of the ancient Christian martyrs. Such things are very moving, but I found a climax to it all when I reached the Chamber of Urns, where only the hearts of a number of saints were kept. These urns, or vases, were of earth, baked brown and hard. One was only supposed to read the inscriptions on the outside and be satisfied with that, but I was not. I wanted to see what had become of the heart sealed up and set away so many centuries before. One was the heart of a martyred Aloysius — the sixth or seventh, I believe. I endeavored to buy the guide to open it for me, but, failing in this, I paid him to let me open it. Upon this agreement I broke the seal and looked in. The heart had changed to ashes. It just looked as though it had crumbled from the shaking I had given it and the effect of the air upon it. The most peculiar part of it was that a stain was left in the basin of the urn, an exact picture of a heart made of blood."

[21 April 1893, p. 7, no. 6]

No. 156.

There is nothing more laughable than to witness the attempt of foreign merchants to catch the eye and trade of travelers in their country," said Carter Cummings, who is at the Lindell. "You see it in Paris, in Rome, in Berne and Berlin, in Constantinople and most every foreign capital and resort where travelers are numerous. Of course, I only noticed the attempts to gain American trade by display signs, hastily improvised and placed out in front of the bazaars. American retail merchants do the same thing no doubt, only we do not see how ludicrous it is because we are not foreign. During the International Exposition in Paris in 1889 French storekeepers put out such signs as 'Latest Furnacings for Gents' in a gents' furnishing store. 'Rost Weal,' before a cafe, was meant to be inviting. 'Frutts and Isses' in a candy and flower store meant fruits and ices—a la American. In Rome, during the

Pope's Jubilee, some of the articles advertised to attract attention were 'Lilley of the Walley,' 'Swett Pea,' 'The Jochey Club,' 'The Luez Canal,' 'Wod Violet' and 'Wery Old Highland Whisky.' What fools these mortals be, anyhow."

[22 April 1893, p. 5, no. 1]

No. 157.

There are many strange and interesting superstitions prevailing in this world," said Magellan Wade, who is at the St. James. "Some border upon the ludicrous, and yet somehow I always find them more to wonder at and pity than to laugh. Sweden and Norway, the land of the ancient north gods, has, I think, more than others, a number of these superstitions. They probably come down from very ancient times—the relics of their ancient mythology which Christianity has not been able to root out of the masses. It is not strange that a nation which could produce a Swedenborg should have some such superstitions going the rounds. One of the most curious of these that prevails in Norway is one that associates the rooster with the dead. A fiction, like that of the ghosts returning to their graves at the first crowing of a cock in the early morning, still holds sway. Many Norwegians believe that a rooster will locate a drowned body by crowing when within a short distance of it on the water. When the

113

lower classes of Norwegians are in search of a drowned body they secure a rooster, and going on the water in a boat row to and fro, fully expecting that the bird will crow whenever the boat reaches the spot where the corpse lies. I witnessed a test of this while in Norway a few years ago, but the cock did not crow, nor was the body found."

[*22 April 1893, p. 5, no. 3*]

No. 158.

"The American Government has a number of shrewd assistants in the Indian scouts of the West, I should judge," said Herbert Bowman, who is at the Southern, on his way to Europe. "I met several of the old-time scouts while out in Wyoming and Arizona. I found them decidedly interesting. I am not good at judging an Indian's age, nor a Chinaman's, either, for that matter. These are two races that can ever deceive me, the majority of them appearing to me to be about the same age. I talked to one Indian scout, however, from whom I obtained a great many interesting notes relative to the old-time scout life, which I hope to utilize some day. What he told me was probably true, because his stories were corroborated by a number of citizens and by written historical facts. I believe he was the first Indian that ever was observed to blush. He was the last one of 100 Government scouts, and

could walk (or run) 120 miles a day, if necessary. All the others are either dead or in jail, having been killed or caught in some treacherous act. His stories were very thrilling, and his memory seemed very clear as regarded names and dates. He was very reticent, however, and did not care to discuss his prowess or that of his comrades. I had to draw him out by degrees, and he really blushed like a girl through his dark skin at the direct questions asked, after he had unconsciously told a little story from out the past. I was thoroughly interested in him and found his judgment to be decidedly clear as regards the little details of this earthly struggle. It seemed strange to me to see an old fighter like that possessed of so much modesty as regards his record and blushing when praised."

[*22 April 1893, p. 5, no. 4*]

No. 159.

"All the village residents of Mejapoho, Mexico, which is situated at the base of Mount Popocatapetl, the volcano, were moved by a strange story in 1885," said Tom S. Mason, who is at Hurst's. "I was there at the time only for three days, and then only at night, because in the day I was out inspecting the surrounding territory. From what I could learn a number of the sight-seers on the mountain had returned to the village on a night in early June and related that they had seen three men leap down into one of the smaller craters on the mountain's side and bury themselves in the bed of molten lava that bubbled and smoked some distance down. Those who related the tale claimed to have afterward visited the crater and looked into it, but that no traces remained of any such tragedy, except a lone white handkerchief marked E. D., which was picked up near by. This they deposited with the village authorities. I was not filled with credulity in the matter, but I examined the linen and listened to how first one of the strangers ran forward a distance of 50 feet while the other two watched, and when he had come to the edge boldly leaped over; then how the second ran and jumped after, and how the third threw something away and followed his two companions. Those who saw it were not Mexicans at all, but travelers from the United States and Europe. They as well as myself left shortly afterwards, with the inhabitants of that small burg deeply convinced that E. D. was the devil, and that he had returned to earth, claimed two of his victims and forced them to leap, alive and well, direct into sheol without judgment. Last year while looking over an old paper file in Portland, Ore., I came upon an article in one of the papers which recounted the mysterious disappearance of Edwin Davis, a citizen of Portland, who left for parts unknown in the latter part of April, 1885, and had not been heard from up to that time, which was two weeks after. A note below stated that a young man by the name of Scott had also disappeared from San Francisco a few days later. There was nothing more to it, and my inquiry did not bring anything further to light than that Davis had never returned. I think of that incident every little while, and recall the Portland end of it, with a vague wonder as to whether the Edwin Davis, of Portland, was the same E. D. who threw away the handkerchief and plunged — the last one of three suicides — over the crater's edge at Mejapoho. If it was not, it still remains a strange coincidence anyhow."

[*22 April 1893, p. 5, no. 5*]

No. 160.

I have often speculated as to what season of the year best adorned a grave yard," said Homer Washington, who is at the Southern. "I have come to the conclusion that it's all gauged by who you have buried in one. Some people find ease of heart and pleasure in visiting a grave yard when the grass is green and the flowers are about in profusion. To such, a grave looks better when shaded by rich bending foliage. It looks most peaceful when shaded by rich green leaves, just moved and murmured to by the wind, and through which the sunbeams stray and dance on the mound below. Such a day suits many just to sink in a neighboring bench and reflect over the happiest days of the past; of other days as bright, with foliage as green and sunshine as warm as that of the present. It suits well then to call back the dead and make them live again in memory until the sorrow of their absence becomes too much to bear. But for my part, I enjoy strolling through a grave yard in winter. I know that the happiest recollection of a day spent among the dead was a few years ago, when I visited my mother's grave in Southern Vermont. It was very cold, and all day long a driving wind whirled fine hard snow pellets around and round, driving them through the bare branches of trees and piling them high in some safe corner, where they were free from the future blast. I remember the ground was not quite white as I stood over the mound, and the crisp brown grass, dead and cold, rattled and whispered with every recurring breeze. The wind blew the snow from the graves and left them all bare— they were too much exposed. I felt as though such a day best typified the sorrows of life. It made me feel more contented than otherwise to know that the loved dead had departed from a world that seemed only too cold and bare."

[*26 April 1893, p. 7, no. 4*]

No. 161.

I was just thinking that this banjo here typifies a condition of human nature most beautifully," said W. C. Taylor, who is at the Lin-

dell. "I've been playing on it until the strings got out of tune. You probably know how the Spanish fandango is played—that is, by tuning the bass in unison with the first string of the banjo. Now, the fifth string here, which is the shortest and sharpest in sound, is in unison with the first string also. That makes the bass and the fifth string both in harmony with the first string. However, the bass and fifth are not in unison with each other. When I sound the first and bass they chime alike, and when I sound the first and fifth they chime alike; but when I sound the bass and fifth they are very far from being harmonious. Now, there you have human nature. I was once of the opinion that if I had two friends and they both liked me, why they ought to be good friends with one another. I once imagined that they could not be otherwise, but I found out different from experience, and I see it here nicely illustrated on this banjo. I can just say to myself, now I am the first string, and here is a friend who can impersonate the bass string. Now, he is in perfect harmony with me, and whenever I go anywhere with him, or he calls, we have a delightful, harmonious time. Here is a second friend of mine, in perfect harmony with me. Whenever he calls we have a delightful time. When both of these friends call of the same evening we meet, and they are both in harmony with me, so that we spend a pleasant evening, just as these three strings give a harmonious sound. But my two friends when alone find no companionship in each other's company. They do not chime on any subject — they need me. I can not help picking out these illustrations of my worldly condition whenever I find them, and so I tell you this one."

[*27 April 1893, p. 7, no. 1*]

No. 162.

I was in Chicago on last Thursday when the great wind storm swept over the lake," said George R. Calbert, who is at the Lindell. "You know how it traveled, the rate being given at seventy-five miles an hour. It blew the Milwaukee crib away and swept the lake most thoroughly of everything on it. For curiosity's sake I went up into the Auditorium tower when the wind was at its height. I had to brace myself against the tower wall, it blew so hard, and with my body firmly braced against the cold stone I could distinctly feel the great pillar quiver and rock to and fro in the wind. The city was a sight to see from where I was. A great mass of towering buildings loom up to the west and stand almost like sentinels near the lake shore, as though to guard the city against its fury. Looking out on Lake Michigan was interesting to an exciting degree. The deep, troubled waters had lost their color and their calm. All along the shore line the waves were rushing in with a roar and leaping high above the wall of rocks that guards it. The swift wind caught up the high-leaping, foam-capped spray and carried it far inland, only to dash it to earth and leave it an ice covering on the ground. The long pier that parallels the land a mile out was the scene of an endless confusion of waves. They sprang high in the air as they dashed against it and played leap-frog as they rolled their foamy crests over it. The water seemed like a thousand-headed monster lashed into fury, which rolled and roared and raised its innumerable heads in wrath and terror. I would follow the great white caps away out in the gray, dark water, rolling steadily toward shore — now rising, now sinking — always with the white spray above them, until with one last, long bound they rushed against the wall and roared themselves to rest. It was so fierce and stormy out that afternoon that the clocks in the Auditorium tower stopped."

[*27 April 1893, p. 7, no. 2*]

No. 163.

Did you ever notice that a present is always something that you can get along well enough without?" said Duncan Hanley, who is at the Lindell. "There ought to be nothing surprising in that, for it is so, and apparently has always been so. Take presents — in the first place, every one has a kind of sense that tells them a present ought to be pretty — beautiful, if you will. First of all beautiful, and then useful if possible. The moment a thing becomes useful and some one gives it to you, it is a gift of charity and not a present. Presents are always largely ornamental; they are something you can get along without if necessary and sometimes what you do not need at all. Take jewelry and watches, umbrellas, canes, slippers, neckties—any one can get along without such things. There isn't a doubt about it. No one will dispute this fact. Yet every one calls up these things to mind the moment he thinks of presents. Does any one ever make a present of a pair of shoes? That would be looked upon as a gift of charity. Even hats are barred from the list as being useful—too useful—and any one who is given one is being materially, charitably helped, because a hat saves money. No one thinks of giving a suit of clothes or anything in the line of necessary apparel. Neckties are given, but a man can go without neckties. He can't go without shirts of some kind, though, or a suit of clothes, except in Africa. He can only do without such things there because it's fashionable at present. People will present a watch worth $50 or $200 and think nothing of it, but they would not give a suit in charity, though it cost only half the sum. So it goes with a dozen other things. No one likes to think that any one else will be benefited by what he gives. People like to see others happy, but not benefited. A man can be easily made happy without being benefited, and that is what presents are for. They are given to give joy and

nothing more. Satisfaction is another, quite another thing, and comes under the head of charity."

[*27 April 1893, p. 7, no. 3*]

No. 164.

Whenever I go into a book store I notice that I always build up a kind of delusive fiction about the names of the various authors I find there," said A. O. Dross, who is at the Lindell. "I suppose it's the same with every one. You pick up a novel nicely bound and you read the title at once; then the name of the author. Whenever I read the author's name I always recall the leisure that he must have had to write a novel; and then, again, I always fancy him a man of wealth, who has plenty of leisure to devote to novel-writing, with a choice home near the seashore, a large library to work in, and plenty of scenery about, through which to ramble and gain rest of mind and inspiration. I imagine an author (still looking at the book) to be a man of culture and refinement, with delicate tastes and a sense of gratification in soft, luxurious surroundings; a man who lingers in bed late of a morning and delights in a leisurely toilet of several hours. That may make up some one else's idea of a fop and a dandy, but to me that constitutes the ideal and successful author. Of course I know different; I know that, out of thousands of authors, all but four or five have no such environment. The most of them are poor strugglers, with disheveled appearance and no money to gratify the better tastes which they may possess. I imagine that the poor thin-coated stragglers who stand before every book stall and glance idly among the pages of dusty, worn books, exposed to the elements, must be chained in fancy by some such thought of delightful existence on the part of others. They think of others living comfortably, and they just stay and vacantly long to be well off and happy also."

[*28 April 1893, p. 7, no. 5*]

been more copies of the works of the Italian poet sold in translation and in the original than were previously disposed of in a century. It is not too much to say that in this country the increase of interest in the gloomy Florentine has kept equal pace with that in England. A statistical Frenchman recently made a canvass of the literary women of Paris, who number 2133, and of these over 300 had read Dante in the original, and over 1800 of them had read it either in translation or in the original. All of them seem to consider it the master work of the world."

[*1 May 1893, p. 5, no. 2*]

No. 165.

The Dante craze, as some are pleased to call the eager desire exhibited at present among certain classes to study the works of the noted writer of the Divine Comedy, is productive of some queer results," said R. P. Holland, who is at the Southern. "Recently I saw a complete translation of the Divine Comedy, which had been sent to the Paris Exhibition of 1882. The volume is so tiny that it measures less than a half inch square. It is perfect, however, and comprises 14,328 verses, with 500 pages complete. The popularity of the study of Dante has of late years had an extraordinary growth in my own country, England. In London within the last decade there have

No. 166.

Perhaps the Asiatic type of cyclone, known as the simoon, is the most remarkable phenomenon of earth," began Col. Samuel Knoop, who is at the Laclede. "In my travels about the world I have never as yet observed any such appalling scene as that of a simoon sweeping its course in the distance. Cyclones in this Western Hemisphere are usually accompanied by great masses of clouds and drenching rain storms. The simoon of Asia is quite different. I have stood on the Arabian Desert where my eye could sweep the distant horizon in every direction without encountering one object to vary the monotony of the scene. Over this vast sea of glowing sand it seemed as though not so much as a breath of air was straying. In such dull oppressive moments the natives were sure to perceive the first premonition of the awful simoon. Such knowledge was of little avail, however, for on that wide limitless stretch of inland sea, like the great bosom of the ocean, one place was as safe as another. The great sand storm would come and sweep its way without any definite path and with no prospect of any sudden variation from its course. Here we have a storm heralded by fierce winds, clouds, lightning and thunder. On the great desert of Arabia the simoon is heralded by nothing more than a small, dark speck in the distant sky. As this approaches the atmosphere becomes stifling and oppressive to an unbearable degree. The speck in question does not develop into a sky mantel of clouds, but its destructive force is none the less diminished. It sweeps in a patch equal to its width and carries with it numberless pillars of sand that are constantly rising and falling like a forest of swaying topless trees. I never was in one, but I have stood on the desert when one was passing in the distance and it reminded me of the shadow of a cloud passing over a sunlit plain."

[*1 May 1893, p. 5, no. 4*]

No. 167.

I was once the sole owner of a $1 gold piece, which, if I had it now, I would not exchange for $500 of any man's money," said Emery Willets, who is at the Laclede. "It was not the intrinsic or extrinsic value of the coin that I prized, but rather because of its associations and the manner in which I came by it. At the opening of the war I joined the 19th Indiana Infantry, commanded by Col. Meredith, at Briggsville, Va. Col. Meredith invited President and Mrs. Lincoln to visit the command. On that day we were all drawn up on dress parade, President, Mrs. Lincoln and the Colonel reviewing on horseback. Then I first saw old Abe. The next time I saw the President I was lying in the Seward Hospital at Washington. I had just finished writing a letter, when a commotion set in at the farther end of the hall. A tall, gaunt figure, with traces of extreme sorrow on every feature, slowly wended its way down the ward amid that labyrinth of cots—it was Lincoln. He stopped at many sick beds, and finally at mine. He sat down and said: 'I see you have been writing a letter' (the portfolio was open); 'have you stationery and stamps sufficient to write to the folks at home?' I told him I had paper and envelopes, and that as for stamps Congress had passed a law making it possible to have letters sent and the postage collected of the recipient. In an abstracted sort of way, and as though he only knew that the boys were in trouble and it was incumbent upon him in some way to relieve their distress if possible, he fished out some change. Tossing a gold dollar to the bed he said: 'Use that for stamps only.' I treasured that gold piece. Stamps weren't anywhere alongside of that. I held it for nearly a year, until once in Southern Virginia I went three days on wind-pudding, and then exchanged it for three 20¢ shin-plasters and a square of johnny cake. I have regretted that bargain ever since."

[*1 May 1893, p. 5, no. 5*]

No. 168.

I had the experience-seeker's joy of being one of an assembly of ten persons who witnessed the cremation of the first negro in the world," said Mark Jenifer, who is at the Lindell. "This occurred in Buffalo a few weeks ago when a negro who had expressed a wish to be cremated was brought from Southern New York to Buffalo for that purpose. I learned that as a rule Catholics and negroes object to cremation. The Catholics look upon it as sacrilegious and the negroes view it with a kind of superstitious horror. The relatives and friends present at the ceremonies did not take kindly to them at all, and if the person being cremated had not placed a specific clause in his will to the effect that his body must be burned it would never have been done. There might have been verbal objections even in the crematory chapel, had it not been for the deceptive coffin hold, the catafalque with the false bottom. This false bottom lowered the coffin during the exercises of prayer and song and when there came a general expression on the part of the friends to see the body of the dead it was found that the body had been lowered, cremated and two hours afterward the ashes of it were placed in an urn and sent up instead. The uselessness of further demonstration took hold upon the mourners and they took the urn and departed. I imagine that to be a kind of event in history, being the first of the colored race who willingly had his remains cremated in this very modern and most civilized manner."

[*2 May 1893, p. 7, no. 5*]

121

St. Louis Globe-Democrat

Titled Interviews

OF the numerous anecdotes that Dreiser either made up or took down from actual speakers for "Heard in the Corridors" at least three, Nos. 169–71, apparently too long for inclusion in the regular column, were printed elsewhere in the paper. Perhaps they were written in expanded form at the copy editor's request.

No. 169.

SEVEN RUNAWAY GIRLS

I will never forget a little experience of mine in capturing a runaway girl," said Sergt. John Broderick, of the Chicago Central detectives, who is staying at the Southern. "It was about two years ago last October that an anxious Irish mother rushed into my office and said that her 16-year-old daughter had run away. I listened to her excited story, took a description and assured her that we always found runaway girls. I gave a description of the girl to all of the detectives and awaited developments. Now, there was at this time an old fellow, a professional bum, who knew me well, for I had run him in at least twenty times, by the name of Chee-Chee. He had finally secured my good favor by helping me to find many a crook whom I could never have located. Chee-Chee knew every dive and den in the city. The Irish mother made a great stir of the matter. It got into the newspapers, and every one began to take interest in the case.

"Chee-Chee came into my office one afternoon, about a week after the case had been reported. He slouched up to me as he always did, in a hang-dog manner, and said:

" 'You're lookin' for a runaway Irish girl, ain't you?'

"I said 'Yes.'

" 'Well, I can show you where she is, if you want. Come go with me.'

"I picked up my hat and started with him. On the way he told me that the girl had made friends with another runaway, and that they were both living on Halsted street, near Madison. The girl was stage struck. He had promised to introduce her to a theatrical manager and he proposed I should play that role. To show you how silly these girls were, the one that I wanted had a watch. This had been laying on the table the last time Chee-Chee called, and when he left it was not there. When we entered Maggie exclaimed:

" 'Where is my watch, Chee?'

" 'I ain't got your watch,' said Chee-Chee.

" 'Yes you have,' she laughed; 'the

last time you came it was on the table, and now it's not there. I know you took it.'

" 'No I didn't,' said Chee, and with that he simply joked the matter away. I scared him into giving me the watch afterward, but that's not the story.

"After that little conversation he introduced me as some manager, and I put on a mild, condescending manner and pretended that I wanted girls for the stage.

" 'Now,' I said, 'I want at least a dozen girls. I am going to start out on the road and play all the good country theaters. If I take you along you will have to be good girls, obey me, and act thoroughly respectable. If you don't I won't keep you.'

"My! how that girl promised. Yes, she would be good, and she could get me lots of nice girls, and they would be good, too. While she said this her eyes fairly sparkled.

"I told her to get me the other girls and have them all there next day at 1 o'clock. Next day I picked out four officers and started for Halsted street. I stationed the men over the way, instructing them when I pulled down the blind in the front room to all come over. Then I crossed over and went in. You should have seen the bevy of pretty, giddy girls that were there. Maggie had got seven others and they all wanted to go on the stage. They were all primped up. Their faces were powdered, their cheeks and lips tinted and their hair done up to perfection. I can't help smiling when I think of it. One girl —

a tall, sad-looking, dark brunette — was beautiful.

"I said, 'Now girls, you are all pretty and you just suit me. I am going to take you out on the road. You will all have to be good, act nice and mind me or I won't keep you. Now will you?' They chorused 'Yes.'

" 'Well,' I said, 'I want your names now, and where you live. I simply want them for my own protection. You must give them to me correct.'

"They were very willing. I drew out a tablet and pencil and began to take the list. They gathered about me smiling and nudging one another. They whispered jolly nothings, and constantly commanded one another to 'hush up, now.' After I had the names I stepped to the window and drew the curtain half. Then I heard the tramp of my men on the stair. I threw open my coat and showed my star.

" 'Now girls,' I said, 'you are caught. I am an officer.'

"Such wailing and crying you never heard. Several got on their knees and begged me to let them go. One threw herself on the bed and began to cry. That tall sweet brunette stood perfectly still, and looked scornful. My, but that girl was proud and handsome, but oh, so cold. We took them all to their homes, for they did not deceive me, and for awhile I was famous. I have met all those girls since. All of them have gone to ruin, and are worn out in body already. I have met that handsome young girl several times since. She fell lowest of all. But proud! She is just as proud and handsome to-day as she was then, and that is why she has fallen so low. I tell you there ought to be a home for these girls — somewhere to send them and keep them. A prettier lot of innocent girls I never saw before nor since, who were on the pathway to shame and moral death."

[*23 November 1892, p. 11, col. 4*]

No. 170.

A TOKEN OF DEATH

S omething that has always appealed largely to my credulity and that I never could explain occurred to me, or rather to my wife, some twenty years back," said J. F. Davis, who is stopping at the Laclede, to a *Globe-Democrat* reporter yesterday. "It is a case of genuine spiritual telegraphy as I deem it. I'll make a story of it.

"In 1855 I was married in Dayton, O. My wife was the daughter of a well-to-do farmer who resided in that vicinity, where I was buying wool at that time. My wife was one of three children, and the only daughter. I will say here, and you will see how it figures in my story later on, that my wife was a very attentive and hard-working girl, and I know that her parents loved her the best of all. After we were married we removed to Terre Haute, Ind., and I took charge of a very large woolen mill as man-

ager. My wife's parents, Mr. and Mrs. Schauab, removed to Western Pennsylvania, very close to Red Bank. We did well in Terre Haute. I bought an interest in a woolen mill there myself, built a good home and raised a large family. After about five years of absence my wife desired to revisit her parents and nothing would do but that we must go. Traveling eastward or westward in 1861 was not what it is to-day I assure you. It meant that I must forsake my business for many weeks; that all the family must be taken along for the sake of safety, and that cost a large outlay of money. We paid the visit and I the bills, and finally returned home. At the time of parting from her mother my wife said that she felt just as though she should never see her again. The whole parting scene was rather sad, now that I recall it.

"Well, we returned to Terre Haute, and for eight or nine years my wife corresponded regularly with her parents. Along about 1871 a letter came from home saying that her mother was ill, but not seriously so. Still it worried my wife a great deal and set her to thinking seriously of going home again. The weight of business and family affairs had grown by this time to such an extent that it required constant attention. My family was a large one, ten children in all, and my wife was an excellent manager, so that in view of the constant need of her I was seriously opposed to her going. Anyhow, she wrote a letter saying that she would come home if they needed her, but that she hoped all would be well without. A few days after I mailed this letter—it was in the winter time and snowing—I came home from the mill and prepared to enjoy myself as I usually did of winter evenings. We had supper and my wife straightened things. She put the children to bed, that is the little ones, and we sat alone in the sitting room. I was reading my paper and she was knitting, as she always did, before the fire. About 10 o'clock she stirred in her chair and said:

" 'Do you hear some one walking?'

"I said 'No,' for I didn't. I felt at once that that was a queer question for her to ask, for it was snowing outside rather heavily. It was one of those soft, wet snowstorms, and it would take a rather heavy walker to be heard on a gravel walk. I said, 'Why, it's snowing out. You certainly did not hear any one walk.' Just then she said:

" 'Listen; some one's tapping on the window.'

" 'Bah,' I said, half nettled at what I deemed her odd fancies, 'I don't hear any one.' I arose from my chair, just to satisfy myself and her, and opened the side door to which the gravel path led. I looked, but no one was there. It was simply snowing heavily, and no boot marks were visible. I turned back, fully assured that it was all her imagination. For a little while nothing happened. I got interested in some newspaper tale, and she again rocked to and fro in her chair, when all at once I heard a tapping on the window pane. My wife

heard it, too. She stopped and looked at me with that triumphant glance of 'there, now; I told you so'; coupled with wide-eyed surprise. We listened. It came again—once, twice, three times. I dropped my paper and opened the door. My wife came and looked over my shoulder out into the darkness. There was not a sign of any one, although I had reached the door quickly, and no footprints were in the snow. I remember saying, 'Well, that's queer,' and shutting the door. Then we sat down to discuss the matter. It was rather a serious discussion, I assure you, although I was not and am not now seriously given to a belief in the supernatural. We talked of the matter, I dare say, ten minutes, when all at once my wife said:

" 'There it is again.'

"Before I could realize what it was, a low, mournful sound came from without; not from the ground, I thought, but from the lower branches of a tree that stood a little distance from the door. It was just like a woman crying in most woful bitterness. Oh, that cry was simply awful! It was just a long, low, human wail that seemed to contain the bitterest sorrow. I was almost dumfounded. I thought my wife would faint, but she only sat still, very pale, and looked at me. Finally I got up and went to the door. It was the same story as before. There was not a sign of any one's presence.

"My wife took it at once for what it was—a token. She said that she knew something must have happened at home, that mother was worse or dead, but she could hardly think of that. Four days later a letter came to my office for her. It was not black bound, for they couldn't buy mourning paper that far out in the country, and maybe they didn't care to. But it was from home, and I felt that it must bring news of death. I opened it, and sure enough it told of her mother's end; how at 9 o'clock on the night that the omen came her mother had died from a sudden inflammation, and that her dying exclamation was 'Oh! I want to see Sarah'—that is my wife's first name. I withheld the letter for ten days, or until I thought her nervousness had passed away and that she had strength enough to bear the news. Then I broke the tidings to her and gave her the letter. It was a cruel blow, and it seemed cruel on my part to withhold the news so long; but I still think it was best.

"Not long after, to appease her anger and satisfy her longings, I took her home again, where she visited her father and the grave of her mother. But aside from all that, I firmly believe in tokens now. I have had some other queer unexplainable things to happen since then, all of which have confirmed me in the belief that there is something that passes between those who have strong bonds of affection between them, that in moments of extreme joy or sorrow flies like an arrow with the news, and we call them tokens."

[*28 November 1892, p. 9, col. 4*]

No. 171.

SAVED IN A BURNING HOTEL

I had a thorough scare not long since," said James McElwell, as he drew a chair near a pillar in the corridor of the Lindell Hotel, and gazed reflectively into the face of a *Globe-Democrat* reporter. "It all happened in the village of Sumption Prairie, near South Bend, Ind. I was at that time agent for a large reaper company in Chicago, and had been in the town but two days when the accident happened. Like most villages that I know of, Sumption Prairie possessed but one hotel, and it does not possess that now. The hotel, or rather inn, was a large, rambling affair of frame. It was only three stories in height, and that was a great deal too tall for its age. This hotel had once been, away back in the 40s, a very swell affair, but that was when Sumption Prairie was a 'heap bigger,' as they say over there, than South Bend ever wanted to be. At that time people were accustomed to come to Sumption Prairie to buy, and the place gave itself many metropolitan airs that it has long since seen fit to dispense with. One of those airs that I speak of was the erection of the Sumption House, which was rather a sumptuous house indeed for Northern Indiana at that time. But the advance of the State has changed all these things. The growth of South Bend in the upper scale has lifted this little village far out of the notice of the ordinary traveling public and condemned it to be forever a mere cross-roads station—a place where sugar-cane is pressed, wheat ground to flour and reaping machinery repaired. But as I was saying of the hotel.

"The Sumption House was a low, rambling old frame, with narrow windows and little panes of glass about 6×4 inches in size. All the paint was worn off, the walls of the rooms were discolored by damp and soot and the floors creaked with every step that one took. The hotel bar was simply an extension of the hotel office counter, a very miserable arrangement to which age had failed to add any charms. A great old wood-burner stove stood in the middle of the office and filled the room with heat in the winter time that was stifling. In this place I stopped over night just eight months ago to-day. I came to the village at dusk in the latter part of May. Sumption Prairie has no railroad to furnish amusement for the villagers. In fact it hasn't much of anything, but I didn't walk in. I came by stage, or hack, as they call it, about ten miles southwest from South Bend. This hack was much after the style of a big 'bob-sled' on wheels, with wooden benches stretched along the side and a door in front to throw in such trunks, parcels and mail matter as might be going that way. We had a good team of horses and by 7 o'clock in the evening we pulled up before this old inn. I got out, extricated my grip from some mail bags and strolled in. That was a hotel that was never crowded. You could always get the best room in the house, and that,

too, at the very moderate rate of $1 a day. I took the best room and carried up my grip to the next floor, where the room was located, and then washed for supper.

"These old country hotels may have poor equipments in the way of servants, light, heat and furniture, but two things they do have—and they are bed and board. I have stopped in all classes of hotels throughout this great country, but I must say that country beds and country board in some of those old frames beats anything I ever came across. I washed and ate supper and after reading an hour or so I told the host to call me at 7 the next morning, picked up lamp from off the counter and tramped up-stairs. Now, then, the windows caused all the trouble for me. They were mere pigeon holes looking out on the street below. To raise one half way and leave the door open gave air enough, but in case of fire and anything blocked the doorway your chances of escape were small. I noted all this, but thought nothing of it, thinking that all would be well anyhow.

"At about 2 in the morning I was aroused from the soundest sleep I had had in a long while by a confused blending of sounds. I distinctly heard some one call fire, and of course I prepared to escape, thinking it was the hotel. My premises were right, it was the hotel and the flames were right beneath me. I thought the floor felt hot, but I took time to draw on my clothing, look about for my grip and then start for the door. When I reached there and looked out

I saw it was too late to get out that way. The flames already filled the hall and barred my passage and my room was now filled with a choking, blinding smoke. Then I made a dash for the window. I forced my grip through and flung or pushed it out. I saw that I would not get out myself without knocking out the upper frame work. That was of good oak and as sound as when first put in. I grabbed a chair and pounded it, but I only smashed the panes and the interstices; the frame would not break. Just then the flames began to burn through several small holes in the floor. Every minute they grew larger and the room was filled with a smoky, lurid glare. I did not stop trying, I know. I hardly recollect what I did, but all the time I was moving about. All at once I felt myself falling. For an instant I had a clear conception of my doom. I was falling into seething flames below. Then came a heavy thud, and that was all I knew for awhile.

"In a little time I awoke and felt about. My hands came in contact with damp clay and smashed glass. Above I saw the building still burning. Every now and then a spray of water fell my way. The inhabitants were throwing buckets of water on the fire. I realized then that I was in a cellar and not dead; a place where they stored milk, butter, etc., and where it was always cool. I crawled on into one corner and watched the proceedings. Hot boards and cinders dropped down occasionally, but I managed to ward them off. I staid in that hole until noon next day, when most everything had burnt away, and my anxious wails for help were taken into consideration. The hotel was burnt to the ground. I was the only one supposed to be lost. I lost nothing but my clothes. My grip I afterward found. For myself I was seriously burnt.

"It was fully a month before I got up and around again, but outside of burns and bruises I was sound enough, and now I often wonder how I escaped. I must have alighted on my feet and then toppled over. At any rate a basement dairy saved me, and I regard all dairies ever since most gratefully. They are good fireproof repositories, and the next best thing in a fire, after open space, to flee to."

[*18 December 1892, p. 29, cols. 6–7*]

131

The Pittsburg Dispatch

DREISER'S last paragraphs in the "Heard in the Corridors" vein, Nos. 172–75, appeared in the *Pittsburg* (Pennsylvania) *Dispatch.* ("Pittsburg" was at the time the more common spelling of the city's name.) They were published in mid-May of 1894, shortly after Dreiser had begun to work for that paper. To supply the demand for copy, what he did, simply, was to slightly rework four items he had written earlier for the *Globe-Democrat,* all of which were then printed on the same page of a single issue. Inasmuch as the *Dispatch* had not run "Corridors"-like pieces before Dreiser's arrival, it is possible that he hoped the city editor would institute such a column and assign it to him. However, nothing further of this sort appeared during his seven-month stay with the paper.

No. 172.

ENTRANCED FOR HOURS

"**Y**ou have perhaps written now and again in the newspapers accounts of persons lying in a trance," began Winton Sharp, a guest of the Willey, to a *Dispatch* man yesterday evening. "I'm one of those persons. It's very harrowing to my senses now to read of anyone lying in that condition, being placed in a coffin, stored in a vault, or even buried, before they come to. I have read of where, a few weeks after some recently-caused disinterment, where the body was found face down, indicating a brain-turning struggle and death.

"My experience went no further than 15 hours, I am certain, but that was enough, thank you. The fact is that I awoke one morning quite rested. I recall I had spent a pleasant night in bed, and lay speculating generally, without moving or even caring to open my eyes. Later I concluded to get up. I felt rather dull, but still comfortable. When I wanted to open my eyes I could not. When I willed to put my hands to them they did not move. When I struggled to stir, it was all a struggle of brain. I must have fainted, for after a time I woke up calmly reflective, though fully conscious of my predicament. I listened and could hear, but could not direct my hearing. I willed to breathe hard, but effected nothing. I tried to call, but had no power of voice. Even my lips felt numb and dead, or mayhap I could not feel them at all. Horror again returned. My brain seemed ready to burst with rushing blood and confused thought. Then a second relapse came, and I felt stupefied. I lost anxiety for movement, or even life.

"Alternate periods followed of mental struggle and stupor. In the afternoon I was discovered by my landlady, who came to look after the room. It seemed astounding to me that I should be compelled to lie there and appear as one dead. Her calls I could not answer. Then others of the family came, and a physician. My nose was feathered, and my finger tips burned, but those remedies didn't disturb me at all. I couldn't feel. About 10 the next morning I came round. When I did, it was with a bound. The following week brain fever set in, and when I had recovered, a year of extreme nervousness was added. Even now the thought of a return attack is a dreadful, though often unavoidable reflection."

[18 May 1894, p. 3, col. 2]

No. 173.

THE ARTISTIC LIAR

I would like to be a whole-souled liar," smiled Peter McCord, the well known Eastern water-color artist, as he smoked a cigar in the lobby of the Anderson. "A good, artistic, voluble liar — really, I would. I don't object to an artistic liar, so long as he prevaricates consistently. The only reason that I don't lie myself is simply that I forget too easy.

"At the period when I thought to become a liar, I was deterred by an example which I will always remember. There used to be an old cuss in our town who came into the store where I was clerking to loaf. He would invariably climb on a stool, heavy as he was, and poise himself gracefully, after which he would chew and expectorate, and lie. He never failed of a good long story — a wild bear story of remarkable adventure. Once he related that he went hunting on a balmy, sun-shiny, soft spring morning and hunted all day. He lingered over each detail pedantically, and described with minuteness the color of his game, the number of prongs on the great buck's antlers that he shot as a climax to his field day, the presence of certain red squirrel, etc.

"He told his story so carefully, and yet so naturally, that for once it impressed me as being so. I was entranced. I didn't care whether it was a lie or not, because it was so esthetically definite; but he wound up his tale by saying that the only reason he did not bring home all that game was simply because the load would have made him break through the heavy snow crust, and he couldn't walk that way."

[18 May 1894, p. 3, col. 2]

No. 174.

THE CURE OF CRIME

"Isn't it pretty near time," said Scharrman T. Ellis, who is stopping at the Monongahela, "that something was being done toward educating the criminal classes? I've seen so much of criminal correction and so little of actual good resulting from it. By what system of mental equity do people live along, the while not endeavoring to strengthen the minds of criminals by proper example and enforced study, but rather to weaken and break down their bodies so as to incapacitate them from further wrongdoing?

"I say this because I think the present penitentiary, and in most States convict lease system, is wrong, and nothing more than a body-wrecking system. I have even heard criminals, who had long been schooled in evil, complain, and for once in truthful earnest assert that they had never an opportunity to learn anything. I have also heard younger men of the same class — mere boys on the road to ruin — ask of the criminal authorities to be taught.

"Not over a week ago a young fellow came before a New York Criminal Court Judge to be sentenced for burglary. When the penitentiary was named he pleaded, 'Can't you make it house of correction, Your Honor? I'd like to go some place where I can learn something.' There is no getting 'round the issue. Something, everything must be done for criminals in the way of education or they will always remain criminals."

[*18 May 1894, p. 3, col. 4*]

No. 175.

FAITH IN A PIG

"The most remarkable thing that has ever happened to me," said Paul Dresser, the song writer, who left the Duquesne last night, "occurred four years ago when I was yet a victim of dyspepsia. Mine was a bad case, I assure you. Oh, I was all broke up. Food, in most forms, was abhorrent, and I walked around actually meditating the hereafter and its possibilities. Some time passed and I grew worse. I saw myself a physical wreck, and try as I might, I could not revive ambition.

"Finally, down in Arkansas, I encountered an old colored grandma, who said I would recover if I would go to a certain farm, and three times a day cast a brown ear of corn to a white pig, remaining to hear it eat. I do not believe in rude fancies, but dear me, I was so sick I was willing to do anything. Accordingly, I bought a white pig of her, and secured a pen for it within the limits of the farm mentioned. Daily I made the trip with an ear of brown corn in my pocket, and listened to the white pig eat. Well, sir, after a few days, do you know the sound of that pig crunching and sucking after those corn grains made me hungry. I enjoyed the sensation so much it made me ravenous. When I returned from my walk I wanted to and could enjoy eating. I continued visiting that white pig for months, when I was rather able bodied again. The whyness of it don't worry me in the least. I'm well, and that's enough for me."

[*18 May 1894, p. 3, col. 4*]

Notes

The principal sources of biographical information used in the preparation of the attribution and textual notes are

Dreiser, Theodore. *Dawn.* New York: Horace Liveright, 1931.
_____. *A Hoosier Holiday.* New York: John Lane, 1916.
_____. *Newspaper Days.* New York: Horace Liveright, 1931. (The earlier printings are entitled *A Book About Myself.*)
_____. *Twelve Men.* New York: Boni and Liveright, 1919.
Elias, Robert H. *Theodore Dreiser: Apostle of Nature.* Emended ed. Ithaca, N.Y.: Cornell UP, 1970.
Swanberg, William A. *Dreiser.* New York: Scribner's, 1965.

In addition to the *OED* and *Webster's Second* and *Third International Dictionaries,* information was drawn from the following specialized reference works:

Bartlett, John. *Familiar Quotations.* 14th ed. Boston: Little, Brown, 1968.
Berrey, Lester V. and Melvin Van Den Berk. *The American Thesaurus of Slang.* 2nd ed. New York: Crowell, 1952.
Biographical Directory of the American Congress 1774–1961. Washington, D.C.: GPO, 1961.
Sobel, Robert and John Raime, eds. *Biographical Directory of the Governors of the United States.* Westport, Conn.: Meckler Books, 1978.
Webster's Biographical Dictionary. Springfield, Mass.: G. & C. Merriam, 1972.
Wentworth, Harold and Stuart Berg Flexner, eds. *Dictionary of American Slang.* 2nd ed. New York: Crowell, 1975.
Who Was Who in America. Chicago: A. N. Marquis, 1943–81.

Attribution Notes

WHEN only a page reference to *Newspaper Days* is given, a sufficient justification for attribution is to be found there. Note that the alternate title *A Book About Myself* was used for the first six printings instead of Dreiser's preferred title, but that, regardless of the title, the pagination is unchanged in any of the printings using the original Boni & Liveright plates. "Probable" designates those items for which strong circumstantial evidence points to Dreiser's authorship but which lack the "hard" evidence of an absolute identification by Dreiser himself or by someone else in a position to know or of internal elements that conclusively establish his authorship.

The following items are found in File 86 of the University of Pennsylvania Dreiser Collection and are therefore not deemed to require attribution notes: 34 through 36, 57 through 60, 63 through 77, 80 through 92, 94 through 98, 100 through 105, 109 through 119, 124, 128 through 147, 151 through 168.

No. 1. Probable. Dreiser certainly wrote "About the Hotels" of 27 October (Nos. 2–4), and he could have written this as well inasmuch as when he began providing copy a few weeks later for "Heard in the Corridors" at the *St. Louis Globe-Democrat,* he frequently interviewed—or pretended to interview—people from Indiana towns, like Evansville, where he himself had lived. No. 1 may be connected in some way with the interviews he gathered this same week in the hire of a *Globe-Democrat* reporter who was covering the dedication ceremonies of the Columbian Exposition (*Newspaper Days,* pp. 81–82). Brief columns entitled "About the Hotels" appear twice in the *Globe* prior to the appearance of No. 1: 14 September, p. 2, col. 3, and 17 September, p. 2, col. 6. These consist of two interviews each. While Dreiser may of course have written them, neither contains any internal evidence to support ascription to him.

Nos. 2–4. Dreiser's authorship is established by the use of names and by the subject of No. 4. William Yakey and Howard Hall, his Indiana University classmates, figure in *Dawn,* pp. 383 and 391. The former is there called William Levitt but is identified as Yakey by Robert Elias in *Theodore Dreiser: Apostle of Nature,* p. 27, and by

William A. Swanberg in *Dreiser,* pp. 28–31. The identity of A. P. Corwaith is unknown, but the name occurs again as *Adam Corwaith* in No. 55. R. L. Jeffery's cave adventure is essentially the one Dreiser himself had (*Dawn,* pp. 403–8). No other hotel interview columns appear after this one in the 1892 volume of the *Globe* owned by the Chicago Public Library, a fact that supports the conjecture that Dreiser moved to St. Louis on Sunday, October 30.

Nos. 5–18. *Newspaper Days,* pp. 81–82.

No. 19. Probable. The preceding summer Dreiser had helped cover the Democratic Convention for the *Globe,* during which time he may have heard this anecdote or may himself have encountered Dr. Walker.

No. 20. Probable. In a vein of fantasy unlike anything that had appeared in "Corridors" during the ten months before Dreiser began contributing to it, this anecdote and No. 21 sound like the kind he says he delighted to invent. *Newspaper Days,* p. 134.

No. 21. Probable. See attribution of No. 20 and compare with Nos. 119 and 172.

No. 22. Probable. The faithful-dog theme is analogous to that of No. 13, which is unquestionably Dreiser's. A misogynic attitude, while certainly not characteristic of Dreiser himself, is expressed again in No. 24, which very probably was written by him.

No. 23. Probable. In view of Dreiser's oft-expressed veneration of his own mother, the uniformly sympathetic portrayal of mothers in his fiction, and the locale of this story, his authorship seems likely.

No. 24. Probable. Stories with Indiana backgrounds are infrequent in "Corridors" during the ten months before Dreiser joined the *Globe-Democrat*—fewer than twenty out of more than nine hundred. With his arrival, however, they become rather more common, twenty-three appearing among some eight hundred during his six months with the paper. When, like this one, they refer to areas of Indiana he was familiar with, his authorship is strongly implied. The romantic element in this story makes it seem even more likely to be his. See the attribution of No. 20.

In "The Country Doctor" in *Twelve Men,* pp. 127–28, mention is made of Id Logan, an old hermit living near Warsaw, Indiana, when Dreiser was growing up there. He may have been the model for this sketch.

No. 25. Probable. See attribution of No. 24. Perhaps this is an early expression of Dreiser's interest in the Quakers that culminated in his 1946 novel *The Bulwark*.

No. 26. Probable. This anecdote bears a marked resemblance to one about the Dreiser family's Warsaw, Indiana, doctor in *Twelve Men,* pp. 117–18.

No. 27. Probable. Uttered by the speaker of No. 26, these comments express an interest in the physical properties of money that is something of a Dreiserian characteristic. See his article "Our Fleeting Shekels," *Pittsburg Dispatch,* 26 August 1894, p. 2, cols. 4–5.

No. 28. Probable. The speaker's observation on the crucial role of luck in human affairs is illustrated repeatedly in Dreiser's fiction.

No. 29. Probable. Perhaps these remarks express Dreiser's attitude toward marriage following the recent breakup of his romance with Lois Zahn of Chicago, to whom he had almost been engaged. See *Newspaper Days,* pp. 126–28 and 198–99 (where she is called Alice Kane). See also No. 83 for another antipathetic comment on marriage.

No. 30. Probable. Very similar in tone and theme to No. 111, which is definitely Dreiser's.

No. 31. Probable. See attribution of No. 24 and compare with No. 16. Bedford is a short distance from Bloomington, where Dreiser attended Indiana University, 1889–90.

No. 32. Harry Hall is undoubtedly the Howard Hall of *Dawn* (pp. 391–92), a law student from Michigan who befriended Dreiser at Indiana University. Lonely graveyards are a recurring topic in these pieces. See Nos. 2, 13, and 160.

No. 33. Probable. The Cook County morgue is the subject of "Fate of the Unknown," appearing in the *Chicago Daily Globe* 11 September 1892, p. 3, col. 1, and very likely written by Dreiser. Other morgue stories possibly by Dreiser are "Chamber of Horrors," *St. Louis Republic,* 7 November 1893, p. 6, col. 4 and "In Old Hancock Street," *Pittsburg Dispatch,* 18 July 1894, p. 3, cols. 3–4.

No. 37. Probable. David Starr Jordan, president of Indiana University during Dreiser's attendance, is mentioned in *Dawn,* pp. 370 and 377. See No. 127.

No. 38. Probable. The role of instinct and conditioning as determinants of behavior was of continuing interest to Dreiser and is touched on frequently in his fiction. See No. 138, which is unquestionably his, for further discussion of animal instinct. Estey's study habits in college may have been those of Dreiser himself, who, incidentally, implies that even by the time he had come to St. Louis he still did not own a watch. See *Newspaper Days,* p. 124.

No. 39. Descriptions of bird flight and references to crows abound in Dreiser's writings. See *Dawn,* pp. 265–66 for a passage that has some close resemblances to this item.

No. 40. Paul Dresser's name establishes Dreiser's authorship. See Textual Note for No. 13.

No. 41. Probable. The occurrence of this anecdote in the same column with that of Paul Dresser strongly suggests that another Dreiser — Theodore's younger brother Edward Minerod — is here being pressed into service, too. At Christmastime were Dreiser's thoughts running on home and his two favorite brothers?

No. 42. The Silver Lake, Indiana, locale — mentioned extensively in *A Hoosier Holiday,* pp. 327–34, and in *Dawn,* pp. 235–42 — establishes Dreiser's authorship.

No. 43. Dreiser has here appropriated the first initial and last name of his former sweetheart Lois Zahn, the "Alice Kane" of the published version of *Newspaper Days.* But he makes his speaker a man, presumably because women — real or imagined — were almost never interviewed in "Corridors" during 1892–93 and because the activities ascribed to L. U. Zahn would not have befitted a well-bred young woman of the time. The mood of loneliness and melancholy expressed here is rather like that in Lois's letter to Dreiser quoted in *Newspaper Days,* p. 127.

No. 44. John Maxwell was a *Chicago Globe* copy editor who is mentioned frequently in *Newspaper Days.* Dreiser himself was twice a collector for easy-payment firms in Chicago. See *Dawn,* pp. 567–71 and *Newspaper Days,* pp. 16–18.

No. 45. Horace Croxton may be Harry Croxton, a friend of Dreiser during his Warsaw, Indiana, days, mentioned in *A Hoosier Holiday,* p. 293; the professor sounds very like the Rev. Amzi Atwater, vice-president of Indiana University, who is characterized in *Dawn,* pp. 415–16.

No. 46. Probable. See attribution of No. 24. The will-o'-the-wisp figures in No. 6 also. Dreiser's play *The Blue Sphere* uses one in conjunction with a railroad train.

No. 47. See *Dawn,* pp. 403–8 and No. 4.

No. 48. Probable. "Thralls" occurs in *A Hoosier Holiday,* p. 298, and *Dawn,* p. 251, as the name of a house in Warsaw, Indiana, where the Dreiser family lived happily for a short period. "Eugene" was a name Dreiser apparently fancied, giving it later to his autobiographical hero in *The "Genius."* The ideas expressed here sound like the sort he might have heard from Christian Aaberg, an intellectual and worldly coworker at a Chicago wholesale hardware firm. See *Dawn,* pp. 341–46, and No. 65.

No. 49. Probable. Compare with No. 33.

No. 50. Probable. The natural, inherent inequality of men is a characteristically Dreiserian theme. In *Dawn,* p. 108, he asserts that he realized early in life that the "creative forces . . . are certainly to blame" for "social injustice" and "economic maladjustment."

No. 51. Based on Dreiser's memory of his boyhood in Evansville: "In the centre of a great common near the heart of the city, a public library was being erected, the bequest of a deceased resident. It was of a beautiful, creamy sandstone and of not unpleasing design, and from time to time I watched with interest the placing of these blocks into one harmonious whole. Its arched doors and fluted columns and cornices remain with me to this day." *Dawn,* p. 136.

No. 52. Russell Ratliff is identified in *A Hoosier Holiday,* p. 503, as one of Dreiser's fellow students at Indiana University. He is called Russell Sutcliffe in *Dawn,* pp. 393–98.

No. 53. In a passage relating to his family's Warsaw, Indiana, doctor, Dreiser says: "Once I fell out of a second-story window at three o'clock in the morning, walking in my sleep . . ." *Dawn,* p. 262.

No. 54. Probable. The blend of spiritualism and science in this piece would certainly have appealed to Dreiser, who always took an interest in any effort to explain extrasensory and apparently supernatural phenomena in realistic terms. The use of material borrowed from another newspaper story is like what he does in Nos. 9 and 62. See the Textual Notes for those items.

No. 55. The occurrence of the name A. P. Corwaith in No. 3 confirms Dreiser's authorship.

No. 56. This anecdote bears a remarkably close, if embryonic, resemblance to Dreiser's famous short story "The Lost Phoebe," first published in *Century* of April 1916.

No. 61. Probable. This and the following item come from the "Corridors" column which Dreiser, much to his disappointment, found himself reassigned to write immediately after his impressive scoop in covering the Wann, Illinois, train disaster, 21 and 22 January. See *Newspaper Days,* pp. 156–69. He had hoped now to be assigned to cover "great tasks" only. Of the nine items appearing in this day's column – all of which may be his – Nos. 61 and 62 are the most interesting.

No. 62. Probable. See attribution of No. 61.

No. 78. Probable. Dreiser was fascinated with birds (particularly the crow), references to which abound in his writings. See Nos. 2, 32, 34, 39, and 75.

No. 79. Probable. This item was occasioned by the death of De Mille three days earlier and probably by the performance in St. Louis at this time of his play *The Danger Signal* in which Paul Dresser had a principal role. Wesley Sisson may have been a member of the company, or perhaps the name was used to mask Dresser himself.

No. 93. Probable. Dreiser could easily have gathered this anecdote in the course of covering the local theaters, a daily assignment for which he had recently volunteered. *Newspaper Days,* pp. 170–73.

No. 99. Probable. This item occurs in a column between two others that are unquestionably Dreiser's and makes an ironic contrast of the rich and the poor that is characteristically Dreiserian.

No. 106. A reference in *A Hoosier Holiday,* p. 295, to the "Harry Oram wagon works" of Warsaw, Indiana, establishes Dreiser's authorship.

No. 107. Probable. The young Dreiser of the 1890s who is portrayed in *Newspaper Days* as a hungry aspirant to wealth and fame could easily have voiced this defense of luxury. It might almost be taken as a statement of one of the principal themes of *Sister Carrie.*

No. 108. A reference in *A Hoosier Holiday,* p. 293, to " 'Mick' or Will McConnell," a boyhood friend in Warsaw, Indiana, establishes Dreiser's authorship.

No. 120. Probable. Perhaps one of the "romantic, realistic, or lunatic" stories Dreiser says he was accustomed to making up for the "Corridors" column, this is like other things he wrote that deal with tokens of approaching death. See Nos. 6 and 170. Moreover, the telling occurs in the Lindell, Dreiser's favorite hotel.

No. 121. Probable. The subjects of memory and song writing, the setting of the Lindell Hotel (Dreiser's favorite location for these paragraphs), and perhaps even the allusion to a rocking chair before the fire (lines 16–17) all point beguilingly to Dreiser's authorship.

No. 122. Probable. See attribution of No. 24. The southern Indiana locale, the Catholic element, and, in view of Dreiser's antipathy for the Church, the skeptical concluding sentence make his authorship of this anecdote very likely.

No. 123. Probable. This may be one of the "lunatic" stories Dreiser remembered having written for "Corridors." See attribution of No. 20.

No. 125. Probable. Maddox's disdain for vegetarianism may reflect the actual sentiments of Dreiser himself, who had belonged to a vegetarian dining club at Indiana University, or those of William Yakey, a friend of his there. See *Dawn*, pp. 394 and 453, where he is called William Levitt.

No. 126. Probable. At about this time Dreiser and his friend Dick Wood were exploring St. Louis's Chinese neighborhood and patronizing its restaurants. *Newspaper Days*, p. 189. In *A Hoosier Holiday*, p. 81, a similar disdain for strong American tea and a preference for the "weak, clear" kind are expressed.

No. 127. Probable. The name David S. Jordan has strong Dreiserian associations. See attribution of No. 37.

No. 148. Probable. This is altogether in the vein of other fishing stories that are definitely by Dreiser. See Nos. 64, 87.

No. 149. Ascribable because of its similarity in topic and tone to "The Old 10:30 Train," a printed poem identified as "By Theodore Dreiser," preserved in File 86, Dreiser Collection, University of Pennsylvania, on a scrapbook page containing nineteen "Corridors" items. Where this poem was printed has not been determined, but its placement on this page and the quality of paper on which it is printed suggest some 1893–94 periodical, perhaps Reedy's *Mirror*. It may be the first publication bearing Dreiser's correct name.

> It's raining out again to-night,
> A dismal, pelting rain,
> That drives against my window
> With a dripping, and again
> With a rattling, stormy fury
> Sheets of water, waves of gray
> Made more grewsome by the thunder
> And the lightning's livid play;
> It brings to me the gloom of life,

> An odd, most welcome pain
> To listen to the whistle of the old 10:30 train.
> With all this storm without, and me
> A sitting here alone,
> With all the distant past in view
> Its evil to atone,
> With chin on hand I wonder how
> I'd feel if I could be
> A boy again, with mother near
> Me praying at her knee.
> How all the cares of life would fade
> If I could hear again
> The whistle of that old 10:30 train.

This poem was reprinted in *Tom Watson's Magazine,* 1 (March 1905), p. 96, under the pseudonym "Marion Drace."

No. 150. Probable. This is simply an expansion of No. 127, which in all probability is Dreiser's.

No. 169. This anecdote can be confidently ascribed to Dreiser because Sergeant John Broderick also figures in two stories he wrote for the *Chicago Globe* as part of a series exposing some crooked auction shops: "Fakes," 10 October 1892, p. 1 and "Fakes," 18 October 1892, p. 1. It has the typical "Corridors" format but was probably too long to fit into the regular column.

No. 170. Close parallels between the circumstances of J. F. Davis's courtship and early married life and those of John Paul and Sarah, the parents of Dreiser, leave no doubt that this story is his. (See William A. Swanberg, *Dreiser,* pp. 3–5.) The spelling *Schauab* (line 16) may be Dreiser's effort to thinly disguise his mother's maiden name, *Schanab,* or it may simply be a typographical error. Cast in typical "Corridors" format, this anecdote was obviously too long to include in the regular column.

No. 171. Probable. Analogous in length and form to Nos. 169 and 170, which are unquestionably by Dreiser. The Indiana locale suggests his authorship as well. Expanded hotel-corridor narratives of this sort are not found in the *Globe-Democrat* in the eight-month period preceding his joining the staff nor in the year following his resignation.

No. 172. A reworking of No. 119.

No. 173. A reworking of No. 141.

No. 174. A reworking of No. 144.

No. 175. A reworking of No. 140.

Textual Notes

No. 1. *1* Thomas E. Garvin] Identified as one of the Indiana commissioners of the National Commission of the Columbian Exposition. *History of the World's Fair,* ed. Major Ben C. Truman et al. (Chicago, 1893), p. 48.

No. 5. *1* Gov. Merriam] William Rush Merriam (1849–1931), Republican governor of Minnesota 1889–93.

No. 6. *1* "A queer incident . . .] This anecdote is in essence the same as one attributed to Dreiser's mother in *Dawn,* pp. 6–7. While at her brother's farm in northern Indiana, she wished, in a momentary fit of resentment over the burdens of a too-early motherhood, that she or her young sons were dead. Immediately three will-o'-the-wisps came dancing out of a nearby woods, an augury to her that her boys were going to die—as indeed they did within the next three years. Dreiser mentions Silver Lake, Indiana, as the home of relatives of his mother in *A Hoosier Holiday,* pp. 327–29, and in *Dawn,* pp. 180 and 235–42. Pages from the Dreiser family Bible, discovered by Dr. Neda Westlake in the University of Pennsylvania Dreiser Collection, indicate that the names and death dates of the first three children were James or Jacob, d. 24 February 1854; George, d. 30 July 1855; Xavier or Xavery, d. 13 July 1857. All three died in Terre Haute, Indiana.

No. 7. *9* Cardinal Gibbons . . . Cahensley] James Gibbons (1834–1921). Created cardinal 1886. Chancellor of Catholic University (Washington, D.C.) from its founding in 1888 until his death. Widely respected for his judicious policies and devotion to American institutions.

Patrick John Ryan (1831–1911), a renowned and popular orator and preacher, was appointed Archbishop of Philadelphia in 1884. In spite of Catesby's allegation, Ryan is not cited in the *DAB* or *New Catholic Encyclopedia* as among the American clergy who opposed "Cahenslyism."

Peter Paul Cahensly (1838–1923) was a German Catholic lay leader who founded a society for the protection of European Catholic emigrants to the United States. In the early 1890s much controversy arose in American Catholic circles over a petition Cahensly's group had addressed to Pope Leo XIII calling, among other things, for the appointment of priests of the same nationality as the parishioners and for parochial schools where the mother tongue would be taught.

Dreiser may have been pleased to include this interview because of his own unhappy boyhood experiences in German parochial schools. See *Dawn,* pp. 128–31.

No. 9. *1* The name of Breckinridge . . .] Dreiser apparently borrowed this anecdote from the story, "Knew He Was a Presbyterian," that appeared in the *Chicago Daily Tribune,* 20 October 1892, p. 3, col. 5:

A pleasing little episode took place yesterday afternoon in the corridors of the Virginia Hotel in which members of two historic American families drawn here to the World's Fair met, shook hands, and exchanged pleasantries.

Gen. J. C. Breckinridge, Inspector-General of the United States army, who, by the way, is a brother of the Hon. W. C. P. Breckinridge of Kentucky, stood talking with Lieut.-Gov. Bestow of Iowa when in strode a tall, gray-bearded man, straight as an arrow, and with striking features. Breckinridge said to Bestow: "That man must be a Sherman. He has the family features." Gov. Bestow at once introduced Gen. Breckinridge to the new-comer, Maj. Hoyt Sherman, a brother of Senator and the late Gen. Sherman. Gen. Breckinridge's remark being repeated Maj. Sherman retorted, "Yes, we Shermans all have the mark of the beast on us." After the laugh had gone round Maj. Sherman continued: "You may not know it, General, but your family, too, has an identifying trait. In the minds of many people the name Breckinridge and Presbyterianism are closely identified," to which Gen. Breckinridge pleasantly replied: "That is unquestionably true, and I believe it shines out through our features. Let me inflict a little story on you. I stood recently on the street of a Western mining city. A gentleman came along, stopped, glanced, then turned and darted a steady look into my face. Uneasy under it I said, 'Well, sir?' He said, 'What is the chief end of man?' I thought swiftly back through the forty years during which I had not seen the Shorter Catechism. Memory rushed into action, and I answered him, 'Man's chief end is to glorify God and enjoy Him forever.' He grasped my hand, shook it warmly, and fervently said: 'I knew you were a Presbyterian. I can tell a Presbyterian as far as I can see him,' and the strangest part of it was that he, too, was an army officer."

Gov. Bestow looked at Maj. Sherman and said: "O, I'll buy the cigars on that story." The Major replied: "I'll purchase anything on that," and the three went laughingly away to the cigar stand to burn some wrapped tobacco to the author of the story of the two army officers and the Shorter Catechism.

Who Was Who in America establishes that Dreiser erred in giving the General's name as "John C." See "Breckinridge, Joseph Cabell."

No. 11. *1* Senator John M. Palmer . . .] Throughout September and October of 1892 the *Chicago Tribune* carried on a campaign against Cook County Judge John Peter Altgeld, the Democratic candidate for governor, characterizing him as "one of the meanest, and most treacherous, and most unscrupulous men that ever entered public life in Illinois." ("Mike and His Man," 30 September, p. 8, cols. 3–4.) One of its charges was that Altgeld and Boss Michael Cassius McDonald, the owner of the *Globe,* the paper for which Dreiser was working, had lied to Illinois Senator John McAuley Palmer (1817–1900) in order to gain his support for the nomination and then had treacherously planned to deprive him of his seat in Congress. The fact that the *Globe* was also attacked in these exposés may partly explain why Dreiser included this interview. Furthermore, he admired Altgeld for his "high, clear, dreamy soul . . . and his sympathy for the betrayed anarchists and the poor" (*A Hoosier Holiday,* p. 225), used him later as the model for Swanson the honest governor in *The Titan,* and even contemplated writing a novel based on his life. (See "Theo. Dreiser Cries City Is Backsliding," *Chicago Daily Journal,* 18 March 1914, p. 1, and "Civic Torpidity Retards City, Says Dreiser," *Chicago Daily Journal,* 20 March 1914, Section 2, p. 13.)

No. 13. *3* Paul Dresser] John Paul Dreiser, Jr. (1859–1906), comic actor and song writer, best known today for his "My Gal Sal" and "On the Banks of the Wabash Far Away." Theodore's oldest living brother. He changed his name to Dresser because he "thought this more pronounceable and suitable to his stage life." *Dawn,* p. 112.

No. 16. *1* "Here is a land phenomenon . . .] The fact that Clear Creek is just a few miles south of Bloomington, Indiana, suggests that Dreiser may have based this vignette on a personal observation made while he attended the University.

No. 18. *3* George Siler] 1848–1908. Upon retirement from the ring, he became a famous referee of championship prize fights and a well-known Chicago sportswriter.

No. 19. *31* Dr. Mary Walker] 1832–1919. American physician and advocate of women's rights, which cause she propagandized by wearing male clothing.

No. 23. *1* Stephen Howe] See No. 22.
18 Kerry Patch] A tough, dangerous section of the Third Police District of St. Louis, which Dreiser was assigned to cover immediately upon joining the staff of the *Globe-Democrat.* See *Newspaper Days,* p. 109.

No. 25. *6* the political earthquake] A reference to the recent Presidential election in which Grover Cleveland defeated Benjamin Harrison.

No. 26. *33* Fortunatus] "The hero of a popular European tale, a man who receives . . . from the Sultan a wishing cap which will transport him to any place he wishes to be." *Webster's International Dictionary,* Second Edition.

No. 29. *39* 'He that . . . or mischief.'] From the essay "Of Marriage and Single Life."

No. 30. *37* It is estimated . . . in America.] In July of 1890 the Postmaster General's office had prohibited transmission of *Kreutzer Sonata* through the mails on the grounds that it was obscene and indecent. See "The 'Kreutzer Sonata,' " *New York Times,* 1 August 1890, p. 8, col. 4.
61 With leave . . . of moors.] An echo of Hamlet, III, iv, 66–67: "Could you on this fair mountain leave to feed, / And batten on this moor?"

No. 36. *1* "I once stopped . . .] This anecdote must be derived from the attempt of Dreiser's older brother Al "to launch a small-town minstrel show. . . . For some reason, though, he found it difficult to connect with success, even if . . . he finally did succeed in organizing a local minstrel show and took it to four or five surrounding towns. But the financial return was not sufficient and he was compelled to return to Chicago—a great blow to him." *Dawn,* p. 281.
48 as Bryant . . . dreams.] William Cullen Bryant's "Thanatopsis," lines 80–81.

No. 37. *13* Pasadena, Cal.] Stanford University is located at Stanford, California, near Palo Alto.
20 seemed to hero worship] A lacuna in the source-text occurs between *seemed* and *worship.* The purely conjectural *to hero* makes sense, but *almost to* would fit just as well.

No. 40. *1* "No, thanks," said Paul Dresser . . .] This anecdote appears to be a complete fabrication, since no evidence exists that Dreiser's brother Paul ever worked in a powder mill. He probably was not even in St. Louis at this time, but more likely was off touring with his theatrical company, which did not come to the city until the second week of February 1893.

No. 47. *86* is plenty for me.] A lacuna occurs in the source text after *plenty. for me."* is a logical emendation.

No. 54. *1* "Spiritualism is my hobby . . .] A slightly reworked version of "Spiritualism's Materialistic Proof," *St. Louis Globe-Democrat,* 4 December 1892, p. 24, cols. 6–7:

MUSKEGON, MICH., December 3.—A spiritualist of this city, named Fielding, is slowly dying with consumption, and has a scheme by which he hopes to prove to those still in the material state that his spirit exists after its separation from the body. He went to Pittsburg a short time ago and obtained a large glass cylinder, so constructed that it can be sealed air-tight in a moment's time. In this cylinder he has suspended with fine copper wire two pieces of metal so light that they can be brought in contact with each other by the slightest motion of the air shut within the cylinder. These wires pass through the cylinder, one being connected with a battery and the other with a telegraphic instrument. He has made arrangements for his friends at his death, and just before the spirit leaves his body, to seal him in the cylinder, that his spirit may be prevented from taking its departure, and at the same time enabled by a series of systematic disturbances of the air within the cylinder to communicate with his friends through the telegraphic instrument. If this experiment proves successful his friends are pledged after he dies to unseal the cylinder and allow the spirit to depart and then seal up and bury the remains.

No. 62. *1* "Of course we are . . .] A nearly verbatim copy of "Exhausting the Earth's Riches," which appeared in the *Globe-Democrat* of 8 January 1893, p. 23, cols. 5–6, itself excerpted from V. E. Johnson's "The Transformation of Energy: Joule's Discovery," published in the December 1892 *Westminster Review,* pp. 644–54. The passage excerpted here comes mostly from pp. 652–54.

No. 65. *7* Christian Aaberg] In 1887–88 Dreiser was a stock clerk for a Chicago hardware wholesaler. Among his fellow workers was Christian Aaberg, a middle-aged Danish expatriate who, though a confirmed drunkard and wencher, was widely read in European literature, history, and philosophy. Young Dreiser was immensely impressed with his skeptical, clear-eyed interpretation of American social and political problems. Despite the dismal end allotted to him in this vignette, Aaberg was still very much alive on 19 October 1921 when he wrote Dreiser from Chicago that he had stopped drinking in 1904 and had not had "a day of trouble of any serious nature since." See Letter File, University of Pennsylvania Dreiser Collection and *Dawn,* pp. 341–46.

No. 72. *5* S. C. Oldfather] Dreiser mentions a Warsaw, Indiana, high school friend named Odin Oldfather, the son of a "fairly prominent" man, in *Dawn,* p. 244, as well as in *A Hoosier Holiday,* p. 313.

No. 79. *5* Henry C. De Mille] American playwright (1853–93); father of playwright William C. De Mille and motion-picture producer Cecil B. De Mille.

153

16 James De Mille] Canadian-born author (1837–80).

28 David Belasco] Widely-known American playwright and producer (1854–1931); collaborated with Henry C. De Mille in producing several plays.

No. 85. *4* Austin D. Brennan] The husband of Dreiser's eldest sister, Mary Frances, familiarly known as Mame.

No. 89. *5* Richard Hasick] A pseudonym probably for Dreiser's friend, the *Globe-Democrat* staff artist Dick Wood, who was "never without" a "*boutonniere* of violets." *Newspaper Days,* p. 124.

No. 93. *1* Count . . . husband] The celebrated Polish actress Helena Modjeska (1840–1909) was appearing in St. Louis at this time. *Webster's Biographical Dictionary* gives her husband's name as Charles Bozenta Chlapowski.

No. 94. *16* innocuous desuetude] A catch phrase of the day, derived from Grover Cleveland's message to Congress of 1 March 1886: "After an existence of nearly twenty years of almost innocuous desuetude these laws are brought forth."

No. 96. *36* rewarded] That is, rewarded with punishment.

No. 99. *6* Richard Saunders] This is also the full name of Benjamin Franklin's Poor Richard.

No. 114. *9* wheel] 1890s slang for "craze" or "obsession" (*American Thesaurus of Slang,* p. 179). See No. 118. Used elsewhere in No. 114 *wheel* means *bicycle.*

No. 133. *1* "As a compiler . . .] Croyden's remarks on the evils of installment buying must surely reflect Dreiser's own experiences as a collector of installment payments in Chicago. See *Dawn,* pp. 568–85 and *Newspaper Days,* pp. 16–31.

No. 136. *1* "A friend of mine . . .] Nelson's reflections on the stone hatchet are the sort that could have been made by Dreiser's good friend Peter B. McCord, the chief of whose kaleidoscopic interests at this time was "the study of things natural and primeval—all the wonders of a natural, groping, savage world" ("Peter," *Twelve Men,* p. 10). McCord later published a novel—dedicated to Dreiser—called *Wolf: The Memoirs of a Cave-Dweller* (New York, 1908), which begins with the discovery by a modern man of a primitive artifact.

No. 137. *1* book agent or a peddler] For an account of Dreiser's own trying experiences as a book peddler see *Newspaper Days,* pp. 41–45.

No. 139. *19* Spencer class] A class devoted to study of Herbert Spencer (1820–1903), English philosopher.

No. 143. *21* Tesla] Nikola Tesla (1857–1943), electrician and inventor, had participated in a recent meeting of electrical engineers held in St. Louis. His public lecture and demonstration had been enthusiastically reviewed, perhaps by Dreiser himself, in the *Globe-Democrat.* See "Tesla's Triumphs," 2 March 1893, p. 4, cols. 1–3. Tesla may be the prototype of Bob Ames, the dynamic young electrical engineer who figures in *Sister Carrie.*

No. 145. *18* Capt. Anson] Adrian Constantine Anson (1851–1922), manager of the Chicago Cubs 1879–97.
32 'Monte Carlo' Wells] Charles Deville Wells, whose feats as a gambler were frequently in the news in the early 1890s, was the subject of John Anderson Peddie's *All About Monte Carlo: Extraordinary Career of Charles Wells the Man Who Broke the Bank at Monte Carlo* (London, 1893).

No. 146. *4* Dahomey] This West African country was in the news at this time because it was being subjugated by the French. In the armies of its king, Behanzin (d. 10 December 1906), were troops of women warriors.
38 decollette] The proper spelling is *décolleté,* but *decollette* may represent Goldsmith's or Dreiser's actual pronunciation.

No. 150. *4* J. Templeton Fay] An obvious inversion of the name of Fay Templeton (1865–1939), a famous American musical comedy actress.

No. 166. *44* is none the less diminished] That is, is not at all diminished.

No. 173. *2* Peter McCord] An illustrator at the *St. Louis Globe-Democrat* who became Dreiser's close friend. (See Textual Note for No. 136; *Newspaper Days,* pp. 120–21; and "Peter" in *Twelve Men.*)